SOUL SURVIVORS

SOUL SURVIVORS

 An African American Spirituality

Carlyle Fielding Stewart, III

Westminster John Knox Press
Louisville, Kentucky

Book design by Jennifer K. Cox
Cover design by Alec Bartsch
Cover photograph courtesy of Picture Network International Ltd.

First edition
Published by Westminster John Knox Press
Louisville, Kentucky

This book is printed on acid-free paper that meets the
American National Standards Institute Z39.48 standard. ♾

PRINTED IN THE UNITED STATES OF AMERICA
97 98 99 00 01 02 03 04 05 06 — 10 9 8 7 6 5 4 3 2 1

Library of Congress Cataloging-in-Publication Data

Stewart, Carlyle Fielding, date.
    Soul survivors : an African American spirituality / Carlyle
Fielding Stewart, III. — 1st ed.
        p.   cm.
    Includes bibliographical references.
    ISBN 0-664-25606-6 (alk. paper)
    1. Afro-Americans—Religion.   2. Spirituality—United States.
I. Title.
BR563.N4S776   1997
305.896'073—dc21   97-1729

**To Mother Rosebud McDuffie,
Mary Casselberry, and Jean Stewart,**
whose spirituality has been
a Rock of Ages,

℞

and to all God's people
who live with soul
who have kept the faith

The community from which I come expressed *an-other* attitude, an attitude that confronted the reality of America, not as plastic and flexible, amenable to the will of the human being through hard work and moral fortitude, but a reality, impenetrable, definite, subtle, and *other*—a reality so agonizing that it forced us to give up our innocence while at the same time it sustained us in humor, joy and promise. I am speaking of a quality of the American experience which through its harsh discipline destroyed forever a naive innocence, revealing a god of creation—a god of our silent tears—a god of our weary years. This may be called "nitty-gritty" pragmatism. It is from this kind of history and involvement with nature, humanity, and God that the dense richness germinates out of which profound religious awareness emerges.

> —Charles H. Long, *Significations, Signs, Symbols,
> and Images in the Interpretation of Religion*

The trauma of slavery stripped us, but not of everything. It was the fact of being stripped which forced us to rely so heavily on a world view, that aspect of culture which creates order. That world view, in turn, forced us to make just enough sense of the insanity of slavery, to create just enough of a belief-system to enable us to reestablish on foreign ground that driving energy for a continued vital existence which is the birthright of all descendants of Africa.

Faced with the realities of slave existence, we had to find ways of expressing, energizing and revitalizing the spiritual being we had salvaged from the wreckage of the holocaust—the effects of which were to last for more than 400 years. For unless this spirit was expressed, it could not be renewed. And if it were not renewed, the circle would not be complete and it would die. Out of chaos and trauma of slavery, the spirit of Africa was reborn in the form of the African-American ethos.

> —Dona Richards, *"The Implications
> of African American Spirituality"*

Thus the power that whites sought over the people of Africa was not only the power to hold them as prisoner-laborers for their life and the life of their children's children: even more profoundly, it was the power to define them in North American terms according to Euro-American social, political, and economic needs. Whites in this way attempted to deny millennia of African history, pressing the tragic ironies of European names, faiths, and categories upon the black present, seeking in that and other ways to guarantee black co-operation and submission far into any future created by white racism and greed.

> —Vincent Harding, *There Is a River*

Contents

Foreword

Within the past two decades, a great number of new books on the black religious experience has appeared, many with academic merit. Together, these books have formed a critical mass of contemporary literature that describes different aspects of black religion and identifies some of the significant contributions of God-consciousness and religious practice among people of African descent. Increasing numbers of African American religious leaders and scholars have found an enthusiastic readership who are responding to this exciting and intriguing new literary genre. Nevertheless, despite the existence of this vast new literature on black religion, one still finds a paucity of critical resources that give careful and sustained attention to African American spirituality. Carlyle Fielding Stewart III's *Soul Survivors: An African American Spirituality* seeks to change this woeful situation.

This book is bold, creative, and refreshing in the way it takes up the issue of spirituality. Stewart brings many years as a pastor, community activist, and scholar to the task of gathering historical and cultural data for this volume. The author thus does not attempt to treat spirituality as an abstract, esoteric journey inward or as an exploration of the mystical. Rather, in a more helpful and everyday way, he shows how black spirituality emanates from the matrices of black culture, its socio-historical ethos and worldview, specifically shaped by the horrors of the Euro-American slave trade ("the Middle Passage"), American slavery, and its continuing dehumanizing and often racist aftermath. Stewart challenges fellow African Americans to take heart as we identify ourselves as "soul survivors," but implicitly he urges persons of all racial and ethnic identities to re-evaluate their all too frequent misperception of spirituality among African Americans, demonstrating how such spirituality may illuminate fascinating appropriations of freedom.

Soul Survivors is a most timely offering as we approach the twenty-first century with all the prevailing evidence of moral decadence, social tensions, and the abandoning of both "habits of the heart" and spiritual values. Amid such destabilization, this book asks readers to widen and sharpen the lenses through which they discern black culture, clues to its staying power, and signs of its genius that have implication for matters of the spirit. Within the next fifty years, demographic shifts within our global village simply demand that people gain a new respect and appreciation for historical contributions, cultural nuances, and spiritual insights of others too long estranged and marginalized. In a surprising manner, *Soul Survivors* pleads with us to end the cultural wars and establish more wholesome norms for intra- and interracial reconciliation.

Equally insightful with traditional African religious retentions and spiritual dynamics in African American folk culture, Stewart provides a rich survey of elements found in traditional African religion. He is particularly instructive with regard to how African and African American spiritual elements combine to yield unique coping strategies and prescribes meaningful survival skills for those who languish in self-hatred or border on hopelessness. Whereas James Baldwin once said that if it were not for religion and the Black Church, African Americans would all lose their minds, *Soul Survivors* amplifies the social meaning and spiritual significance of Baldwin's casual observation. Stewart uses a litany of compelling arguments and illustrative citations to demonstrate that a more comprehensive spirituality—not just the Black Church or religion—is to be credited for the many Blacks who, despite all the odds and forces against them remaining sane, still find themselves in the United States of America "clothed in their right mind"!

In *Soul Survivors* Stewart builds on the creative probes that he set forth, in a preliminary way, in his previous book, *Street Corner Theology*. There Stewart suggested in eight powerful case studies a new approach to Black Theology, one that would analyze the operative "God-talk" of African Americans in the diversity of "boundary experiences" that oppression and racism in America so often impose on them. The discrete reflections about life's challenges and their possible relevance to perceptions about God's presence found in *Street Corner Theology* are now given in *Soul Survivors*, a more substantive historical and cultural framework.

I am certain that those who take the time to give this book a careful reading will also find it to be deeply moving and rewarding. Here is the work of an original thinker who synthesizes a great body of literature seldom brought together in order to provoke and challenge us to reaffirm the strong positive features of African American spirituality found in our culture. Yet, *Soul Survivors* concerns itself fundamentally with the unique ways African Americans, despite it all, have stayed on that long road to freedom by giving varying expression to an African aesthetic of the spirit. As one who has known and worked closely with the author over the years, I can say that I am extremely pleased with this book, perhaps Stewart's most significant literary and scholarly contribution to date.

Cain Hope Felder
Professor, Howard University School of Divinity
Chair, The Biblical Institute for Social Change
Washington, D.C.

Introduction

One of the most significant elements shaping the character, culture, identity, and destiny of African Americans is the practice of black spirituality. That we are and always have been a deeply spiritual people cannot be denied, for ever since our genesis in the motherland, when God breathed air into our nostrils and sutured limbs made from clay, our spiritual waters have run still and deep.

We have thus acquired our identity, defined our being, and fathomed the very essence of our nature in spiritual terms. Having an affinity for the sun, we have transversed the planet in the rushing spirits of raging winds and swept the earth in the pelting drops of falling rain. We concur with a paraphrase of the great poet Alfred, Lord Tennyson, "We are a part of all we have met." We all are part of the circle of life. The cultivation and preservation of our very souls has been a central quest of our spiritual striving. Our deep and abiding love of God provides us with a determination to live life fully and spiritually, notwithstanding the "slings and arrows of outrageous fortune."

African Americans are spiritual because we have always given God ultimate adoration for our primal and cerebral powers, and we affirm pure soul force, the spirit of God and spiritual belief as the most vital aspects of our being.[1] Along every furlong of our journey, whether in Africa, the Americas, Europe, or Asia, we have been seers and votaries of the oversoul; a people whose spirit and tenacity, brains and brawn, have laid the spiritual cornerstones of human civilization.

We have thus vouchsafed and affirmed spirituality as the hallmark of our unique identity as a people. Even now it is God, very God, who anoints our steps and forges sacred pathways to human dignity, self-realization, and freedom.

Moreover, in contemplating all the hell we have caught on this planet as people of color, we must have a creative soul force, some *utamaroho* (spirit life of a culture and collective personality of its members), which has prevented us from losing our minds.[2] It is no accident, then, that after centuries of murders, atrocities, floggings, lynchings, rebuke, discrimination, oppression, alienation, exploitation, degradation, and human devaluation, we are still alive—not always well but nevertheless alive and kicking. The fact that African Americans still inhabit this planet, are moving onward, and in Sterling Brown's words, "getting stronger," suggests that we have had a viable relationship with the Creator that has ultimately insulated us from the vicissitudes of time and the terror of our American odyssey.[3]

How did we do it? How did we "come over a way that with tears has been watered, treading our path through the blood of the slaughtered?"[4] What intimations and exigencies of the Spirit moved us onward and upward? How could we have come this far without losing our souls in the doldrums of human decadence and despair?

To survive is one thing. To survive with dignity and hope with our souls and minds reasonably intact is quite another, and it is precisely our spirituality that has enabled us to survive, to maintain hopeful optimism on "slender threads," to keep striving for excellence in all things, notwithstanding our peril and plight.

An unquenchable thirst for God along with a profound spiritual capacity to adopt and adapt to our American experience have been keys to our sanity, solace, and freedom as a people. Had we not possessed an adaptive and expressive spirituality, we would have perished years ago, either by suicidally killing our "jailers" or by wallowing in the dregs of angst, lethargy, and dread, never to rise from the ashes of our despair.

We have come this far *through* our spirituality. We have practiced freedom because of it and not in spite of it as some would cynically have us believe. Our firm belief in God has thus led to a living hermeneutic, an alternative consciousness and being, whose very structures have aided our survival as a people. Because our spirituality gives us a creative and transcendent way of seeing, acting, and responding to the world around us, we have come this far. That we still have sparks of a soul and some semblance of humanity left in us despite fervent attempts to destroy us suggests that we possess a vital spiritual strength that has sustained us through the dangers and hardships of our American experience.

Moreover, it is utterly amazing that we have endured slavery, centuries of systematic racial discrimination, and oppression without despising our tormentors en masse. As Cain Hope Felder has observed, "What have we ever done to some whites to make them hate us so? Given all the grief they have heaped upon us, we should loathe them but don't."[5] Compassion, empathy, and human understanding still prevail for our adversaries, and this is one of the great strengths of our spirituality: freedom from soul-consuming hatred and freedom to choose responses to oppres-

sion and dehumanization that exemplify positive consciousness and ultimately preserve the integrity of the soul.

It is my contention that black spirituality and black culture have created alternative modes of consciousness and existence that have sublimated the anger and dross of white racism and oppression into a positive
soul culture.

A primary thesis of this work is that African American spirituality has
made us soul survivors and is the seedbed of our quest for human freedom. This model of human freedom differs from all others. Its very
essence and nature has enabled African American people to face, confront, and transcend spiritually their social, political, and ontological condition. The efficacy of the African American paradigm of freedom lies in
its capacity to encourage black people to develop a culture of spirituality
and a spirituality of culture where the freedom to create is intimately
bound to the freedom to be. Thus the freedom to create a viable black spirituality, which both embraces and transcends Anglo society, creates a context for the emergence of African American culture. The freedom to create
and determine the nature, trajectory, and style of the self is the direct antithesis of a society that seeks to define, reduce, and determine the inherent nature and limits of that being for exploitative purposes.

The essence of freedom, therefore, is not as socially, materially, and politically necessitated as it is in other paradigms, but it is spiritually and
culturally determined. African American culture and spirituality thereby
create a context wherein the quest for human freedom is not precipitated
and shaped by political and social realities but by the people's capacity to
create hegemonically their own spirituality of culture in response to oppression, thus combatting and transcending its myriad devastations. This
does not negate social and political freedom. It only suggests that freedom
of the spirit has been an essential element in African American spiritual
praxis. It is a first freedom that permeates all freedom in the African
American experience.

The freedom to realize wholeness, spiritual vitality, and develop unique
idioms of a black soul culture through imagination, creativity, and freedom of the spirit is primordially important in a society where political, economic, and social freedoms have largely been denied. This freedom to create a culture, to fashion a uniquely black worldview while surviving the
perils of oppression is one of the most important characteristics of the
African American experience. There is thus a culture—a reality and ethos
that is authentically African American, made possible and sustained by
firm belief in God and the undaunted practice of spirituality and culture as
forces for liberating and effecting positive reality.

While black Americans have not always been geographically or politically free, they have been free enough to have a living, meaningful relationship with God, which makes a profound difference in how they view themselves, the world, and their oppressors. Such freedom provides a liberty of the soul, which is the center of black spirituality and culture. It compels black people to imagine and create, to cultivate internally a culture of consciousness and belief indispensable to their sanity and well-being in American society. It enables them to translate that consciousness into positive social reality. It also influences the creation of a black cultural hermeneutic that is essential to understanding who and why we are as a people.

Unlike some discourse on black freedom in America, which advocates a hostile rejection of all Anglo-American mores and culture, African American spirituality has ingeniously appropriated the positive aspects of the Anglo-American experience. Some black scholars, in a positive attempt to claim their African roots, maintain that African American culture and spirituality are exclusively African in origin and contain no vestiges of Anglo-American influences. The problem with this view is that it belies the pragmatic influences of cultural formation by obviating the ability of the black oppressed to seize their destiny by creatively and intentionally appropriating those folkways and traditions of Anglo culture that ensure their long-term survival. This statement is equivalent to saying that the Hebrews have no vestiges of Egyptian influence after four hundred years in black Egypt, or that no traces of Egyptian religion are evidenced in the practice of religion among the Israelites. It equally negates the virtues of Anglo-American culture, which, despite its politics of racial oppression, retains numerous redemptive qualities.

We contend that African American spirituality has coalesced the best of both worlds into a framework for human existence, and that its genius synthesizes certain aspects of Anglo and African cultures, thereby forming a unique African American identity. The ability to choose elements of Anglo culture and appropriate it for synthesis in African American culture is precisely an important aspect in the African American experience and also, however strangely, exemplifies the power and spirit of black freedom.

Both the viability and volatility of African American spirituality exist in the manner in which it has freely chosen the dynamics and form of its own agenda, thus consolidating its identity, and the manner in which it has appropriated adaptive mechanisms from other "cultural archives" as a basis for self-determination and survival.

Thus we cannot speak of African American freedom, culture, and consciousness without delineating the role of black spirituality in creating and sustaining the creative processes of freedom. The uniqueness of the

African American paradigm lies precisely in the fact that freedom is not simply an external, material goal but equally a spiritual and cultural practice that spawns the creative implementation of a culture soul of the spirit that resists domination. It embodies an alternative consciousness, an oppositional way of seeing and being in the world that affirms those expressions of black culture that cannot be completely domesticated by the dominant culture and society.

This creative process is the sacred fount, the sanctum sanctorum ("the holy of holies") of African American spirituality and culture. How, why, and what we create constitutes the unique aspects of our human condition and is the very linchpin of our sacred strivings for freedom.

Not until I lived in England and traveled to various countries in Europe and North Africa did I begin to see how the sovereignty struggles of other oppressed peoples have been inspired by the spiritual experiences of African Americans. Whether it is Berliners singing "We Shall Overcome" or South Africans reading *Why We Can't Wait*, our legacy of spiritual freedom has inspired millions in their struggle for truth, justice, and freedom.

Ironically, few people, especially African Americans, are aware of this invaluable contribution to the freedom of the world. It is one of the world's best-kept secrets. Since few black scholars have had the privilege of traveling abroad and interacting with other peoples and cultures, some have grasped the significance of the African American contribution. Many have had eye-opening, life-changing encounters that have broadened their understanding of the value of African American spiritual beliefs. I firmly believe that in order for African Americans to know who they are in a larger sense, they must travel abroad to get an appreciation of how they are viewed and valued in the eyes of the world community.

Because of these limitations in the developing of a hermeneutic of freedom, some black scholars have felt the need to revert to other thinkers such as Karl Marx, Vladimir Lenin, Mao Tse-tung, Jean-Jacques Rousseau, or Mohandas K. Gandhi to clarify and qualify the African American viewpoint. This is not a problem in itself, but the truth is that African Americans have a prototype of human freedom that is distinct from all others. The function and role of black spirituality in preserving black soul force and the black culture soul is the differentiating factor. Thus we cannot fathom the African American archetype without explicating the role black spirituality and black culture play in shaping black consciousness and creating alternative modes of human existence.

No longer must black scholars import and appropriate other thinkers simply to legitimate their own viewpoint or because they are oblivious to the hermeneutical and paradigmatic contributions African Americans have made to world freedom. While other writers significantly impact our understanding of human freedom, African American scholars must further identify and define how black spirituality has influenced the formation and practice of black freedom at home and abroad. The purpose of this book is to delineate the central components of this African American paradigm of freedom and to explain how this unique model of spirituality has created the substance and framework of human existence that has aided the soul survival of black people in America.

The time has come to examine and articulate the various aspects of African American spirituality and establish its place among other models of human freedom.

One

The Sources
of African American Spirituality

For years, various segments of the black and white communities have debated the survival of Africanisms in African American life and culture. Melville Herskovits and E. Franklin Frazier have been the most prominent antagonists in this argument. Herskovits affirmed that vestiges of Africa did survive, while Frazier contended that slavery and the experience of American enculturation had obliterated virtually all remnants of African influence.[1]

African cultural influences have affected African American culture, especially through various spiritual practices and religious belief systems. Scholars such as John S. Mbiti, E. Bolaji Idowu, and others have provided thorough analyses of African spirituality and religion.[2] While writers such as Albert Raboteau and Robert Hall postulate the variances between African and African American spirituality, strong resemblances are evident in the way spiritual beliefs are integrated into black life and expressed in ritual and ceremonial forms throughout the diaspora.[3]

African Creation Cosmology

While I cannot possibly delineate these two belief systems exhaustively, I will delineate some presuppositions of the African *cosmology* or worldview that are pertinent to African American spirituality as a practice of human freedom.

One of the salient aspects of African and African American spirituality is the cosmological basis of all understandings of God, which coalesces these two entities into a unified framework. The diversity of African spirituality ranges in the various belief systems from African Christianity to Islam to African traditional religions. The structure and content of these various systems are highly differentiated while the expressive forms of religious beliefs are very similar. Thus in Africa we find a multitude of religions but distinct modalities in the ways those beliefs are ritualized, practiced, and expressed throughout the continent.

Conversely, the African American experience finds diversity not so much in the varieties of religion since the majority of African Americans are Christian but in the expressive forms of the denominations within that religion. For example, the varieties of spiritual expression found in ritual ceremonies and religious precepts may be very different between black Baptists and black Episcopalians. While the religion of these two groups has a unified basis—belief in Christ—the idioms of spirituality in worship and life are largely heterogeneous.[4]

Thus great diversity exists within and between African and African American spiritualities. The philosophical and theological suppositions also vary greatly according to the religious texts, classes, and cultural contexts.

Despite these multiplicities of spiritual belief, practices, and expression, a firm cosmology undergirds and informs the practice of African and African American spirituality at all levels. This cosmology transcends the nuances and complexities of various religious beliefs and practices and is the unifying thread of African and African American spiritual belief systems particularly as it relates to those cultural and theological beliefs that inform the practice of freedom.

This cosmology holds that God, the Divine Spirit, or Nature is the absolute, hegemonic, supreme, primordial reality, which orchestrates, governs, empowers, transforms, and infuses creation with a creative soul force that is the basis and power of life. This means that no material reality or society as a created, secondary realm of this divine reality can ever exceed or exhaust divine energy and primacy. This also means that no human power, individual or collective, can ever invert or subvert the ultimacy of this divine Spirit in the human realm. As one African elder remarked, "God is the first and last word of all our affairs."

Dona Marimba Richards tells us:

> The African universe is conceived as a unified spiritual totality. We speak of the "cosmos" and we mean that all being within it is organically interrelated and interdependent. The Western materialized universe does not yield cosmos. The essence of the African cosmos is spiritual reality. That is its fundamental nature, its primary essence. But realities are not conceived as being in irreconcilable opposition, as they are in the West, and spirit is not separate from matter. Both spiritual and material being are necessary in order for there to be a meaningful reality. While spiritual being gives force and energy to matter, material being gives form to spirit.[5]

Nature refers to the material forms of reality and creation. Spirit is that dynamic, cosmic force that inspirits all creation with movement, energy, and vitality. Nature and Spirit are thus the highest realms of existence and are manifested through God's creativity in the universe.

Perhaps the Egyptian idea of nature, *netcher* or *neter*, which is a synonym for God as material, bodily, or the corporeal manifestation of all physical reality, is closely reminiscent of this African cosmic idea. Spirit is equivalent to the Egyptian *kha ba*, which is "holy breath." This concept was later developed by the Hebrews as *ruach* and the Greeks as *pneuma*. While Nature and Spirit might be delineated as separate realities, they are, according to African cosmology, a unified reality.[6]

Anthony Browder observes:

> From the beginning of time Africans have always had a belief in one God, self-created and all powerful. Upon observing the wonders of universe, man began to see the many manifestations of the one *creator* reflected in all that existed and identified them as aspects of the One, or Netcher. This monotheistic viewpoint saw *everything* as part of the whole. A Netcher is not God, it is an integral part of that which is God.[7]

In other words, while this Divine reality may be manifested in multiple forms at various junctions in nature, society, and human history, Divine Nature and Spirit as a unified reality in African cosmology is the foundation of all African and African American spirituality and translates into divine freedom in the human realm. This cosmic spirituality permeates the varieties of African religious beliefs and practices. It is the undergirding foundation of all African spirituality. The creativity of the Creator and the dissemination of this principle in creation through Nature and Spirit is a salient characteristic of African spiritual belief systems. Thus the cosmological basis of African spirituality includes the process, power, and substance of God's creative capacities in the universe. This creativity extends and translates into the nature, spirit, and consciousness of black people, thus becoming an important part of African culture and life. Thus the hegemony of the Spirit in the cosmological realm translates into an autonomy of the spirit in the personal realm. God is the God of Nature and Spirit, the God of creativity who imbues black people with a creative soul force that sustains their survival and validates their existence. The freedom of God to be God and to create, infuse, and transform reality is therefore bequeathed to humankind.

Thus at the very heart of African and African American spirituality, notwithstanding variations in content and structure throughout the African diaspora, is a cosmology that venerates Nature and Spirit as the supreme moral and spiritual sources of black existence. There is no authority higher than Nature, no power greater than Spirit. The creativity of God is the dynamic force that activates, orchestrates, and consolidates the realities of

Nature and Spirit. This creativity is not only a force of Nature and Spirit but indispensable to the idea of freedom in African American life and culture. We will say more about this later.

The absolute hegemony of Nature and Spirit in African and African American belief systems is the consummate fount of all black spirituality and helps us obtain a better understanding of how it informs African American spirituality. Just as the hegemony (or power) of God can be seen in the spirit of creativity within the cosmos, the autonomy of humankind is preserved in the creativity of humanity within society. This means that God and God alone, through Nature and Spirit, is the ultimate architect and grantor of human freedom to African peoples. This view has important implications for African American spirituality and the practice of black freedom in America.

The Bible

Any serious discussion of African American spirituality as the practice of freedom must also consider the importance of Christian scripture in the identity, formation, and empowerment of black life. The Bible has always had an important role in helping African Americans face and surmount the tragedies and perils of their existential condition. From a Christian standpoint, the Bible is one of the ultimate authorities establishing and evaluating black life in America. Even slaves, when scripturally exhorted by their masters to be obedient, understood biblically that slavery was evil and that God ultimately desired their freedom.

The Bible has thus been used by African Americans as a primary text in the practice of spiritual and cultural freedom. Not only has a liberation hermeneutic been derived from scripture but also adaptive mechanisms that encourage blacks to be intelligent, wise, and buoyant in surmounting the perils of their human condition. Inspiring wisdom and intelligence among black people, it has given them the tools for survival in an oppressive and racist society. The Bible has had a central role in preventing black people from being completely domesticated and dominated by slave masters, oppressors, and other adversaries.

The Bible thus has both *textual* and *contextual* significance. The textual importance of scripture provides black people with unconditional spiritual principles for the practice of human freedom. The word of God ethically exhorts and implores the liberation of consciousness, being, and the community of African American people for the actualization of potential and the realization of wholeness. The contextual significance of scripture provides black people with the conditional praxes (or principles) necessary for the actualization of human freedom in the external realm. While the textual value of scripture reveals the unconditional principles of freedom, the contextual significance discloses the conditions for the praxes of freedom.

The Bible has had both a liberating and a humanizing function in African American life. While the imperatives for spiritual transformation and freedom are scripturally exhorted, so too is the actualization of mercy, love, justice, and forgiveness. Living within this double hermeneutic or biblical parentheses has therefore inspired African Americans to accommodate, adapt, transcend, and transform their social and political condition, which is integral to the practice of spiritual freedom. Whether it is Moses leading the Hebrew people to freedom or Jesus healing the physically challenged and disabled, the double hermeneutic is a powerful source of cultural and spiritual creativity and vitality.

An additional importance of scripture is the way it relationally compels African Americans to remain vitally connected with divine reality. It has created a kind of biblical mode or narrative consciousness of existence that has insulated them from full annihilation. The Bible is one window through which black people experience, interpret, process, and shape their relationship with God. As one saint in my grandfather's church once stated, "It's one thing to have an *opinion* of God. It's another thing to have a *relationship* with God." The Bible nurtures that relationship. The Bible provides the medium for interpreting and practicing the meaning of the divine encounter within the human context.

The Bible has always fostered a relationship with God for black Americans that is vital, unwavering, and unchanging. It has encouraged them to stabilize their human condition and reach some spiritual stasis amid the vicissitudes and uncertainties of life. Amid the horrors and terrors of slavery, Jim Crow laws, racial discrimination, and social alienation, the Bible has been the one true foundation, the one solid rock, the ultimate adjudicating moral authority that has helped black people relocate themselves spiritually and maintain some semblance of spiritual vitality amid nefarious conditions.

The Bible has thus played a vital role in African American spirituality and black freedom. It is the instrument of spiritual empowerment that remains a reliable source of information for black survival. By inspiring African Americans to cultivate a hermeneutic of liberation, adaptation, and narrative modes of consciousness, the Bible has been a central source of empowerment in laying a foundational blueprint for African American freedom. Thus the Bible has had textual, contextual, and relational significance for African American people.

African American Culture

Another important source of African American spirituality as the practice of human freedom is the black experience and culture. We stated earlier that a hallmark of African American spirituality is the development of a black culture soul or cultural archive that informs and shapes the consciousness, identity, and being of black Americans. Spirituality and culture continually create idioms of value and belief where black people are empowered to create, interpret, and express their own mythos and ethos, establishing their own archives of truth and power. Black spirituality thus informs black culture, and black culture informs black spirituality. We cannot fathom black culture without the creative, expressive modalities of black spirituality. We cannot conceive of black spirituality without understanding the influence of black culture on its nuances and narratives, texts and subtexts. The heart of black culture includes the music, drama, dance, sports, humor, literature, spirituality, philosophy, and other disciplines of African American life.

Black spirituality is at the heart of black culture, and black culture is at the heart of black spirituality. Both influence the continual formation of the black culture soul, which is the unifying dynamic of black spirituality and culture. The passion, spirituality, and intelligence of black people culminate in the creation of a black cultural archive that creates and preserves its own truths, myths, and presuppositions. This cultural archive informs and shapes black belief and enables black people to create distinctive modalities of life and culture that are uniquely African American.

The black culture soul is the vital center of existence that functions internally in the lives of black individuals and externalizes itself in the formation of community. It involves a cohesive network of relationships, behaviors, and beliefs that not only shape black consciousness and empower black life but also equip black people with the cultural and spiritual amenities indispensable to their long-term health and survival. The black culture soul is the archive of reality that confers black identity, creates alternative modes of consciousness and existence, and differentiates the soul of black life and culture from other peoples and cultures. It possesses its own lexicon of truth that not only has expressive but redemptive function.

Many people see this culture soul as having only expressive function. Soul is identified with black feeling, passion, and compassion, and it allows black people to express themselves from their true spiritual center. While this is true, in a larger sense this soul functions pragmatically to shape an alternative identity and consciousness by ordering the uncertainties and complexities of life into a viable, manageable framework for black existence. This soul is not only expressive but transformative—it centers black life in existential reality and shapes adversarial forces into liturgies for black survival.

The manifestation of the black culture soul can be seen from the creation of the spirituals, jazz, and the blues, to the unique folkways and mores of African American life and the establishment of social justice. Everything that is genuinely African about black life in America, from the walk and talk to styles of dress and ways of expressing the deeper truths of black being, contains this unmistakable infusion of cultural creativity and identity. This cultural creativity is a vital dimension of African American spiritual freedom.*

Spirituality and
Double Consciousness

We stated in the introduction of this book that a genius of African Americans is the manner in which they have appropriated significant aspects of Anglo culture as tools for survival and cultivated a unique hermeneutic of existence. A hallmark of African American life is the manner in which black people ingeniously assimilated and synthesized the best of the Anglo and African cultural experiences into a meaningful framework for human existence. For example, jazz is the artistic epitome of the amalgamation of European and African musical forms into a uniquely indigenous cultural creation. This reciprocity of influence can be equally seen in other aspects of African American life. Mechal Sobel is correct in observing that white and black America have invariably created each other.[8]

On the other hand, W. E. B. Du Bois's celebrated classic, *The Souls of Black Folk*, delineates the dilemma of the double consciousness that results in part from our transplantation from Mother Africa to our implantation into the womb of a hostile America. For Du Bois, this double consciousness leads to ambivalence or confusion about identity, which further lends itself to social alienation and despair. He explains it as follows:

> The negro is a sort of seventh son, born with a veil, and gifted with second sight in this American world—a world which yields him no true self-consciousness, but only lets him see himself through the revelation of the other world. It is a peculiar sensation, this

---

*Another important influence on the praxis of African American spirituality is the black church. Perhaps no other institution in American society has had more impact in shaping spiritual consciousness and empowering the collective praxis of freedom than the African American church. It is the safe haven where blacks convene to share their individual and collective concerns as a people and community of faith. It has been the only institution in the African American experience that has maintained relative autonomy from the domesticating influence of white oppressors and overlords. James Cone, Gayraud Wilmore, and other black scholars have spoken thoroughly to these issues. We will say more about the black church's influence in a later chapter.

double consciousness, this sense of always looking at one's self
through the eyes of others, of measuring one's soul by the tape of
a world that looks on in amused contempt and pity. One ever feels
this twoness—an American, a Negro; two souls, two thoughts,
two unreconciled strivings; two warring ideals in one dark body,
whose dogged strength alone keeps it from being torn asunder.[9]

This doubleness has led to psychological dislocation and a denigration of
black life and identity, according to Du Bois. The problem is that blacks
have been conditioned to look at themselves through the eyes of their oppressors and to devalue themselves as inferior to them.

Marimba Ani says:

The European self-image is a "positive" one in terms of normative
European behavior; it is functional in terms of European goals. It
does its job well. A negative conception of "other" is the basis
upon which Europeans build their image of other peoples; i.e., the
conceptual construct is provided by the nature of their culture,
and Europeans create vivid images with which to fill it.[10]

But it is also true that this doubleness has created alternative ways of
viewing and acting in the world. While some might see the reality of
twoness as a curse of racism and cultural disintegration, my contention is
that this consciousness has also invariably created a kind of psychological
dexterity, a creativity and capacity to interpret the world and adapt one's
being to a variety of circumstances and conditions. Adaptation and creativity are important tools for survival for African American people.

As one of my theology professors observed, any people having to think
twice about being in the world are perhaps far more adept at adapting
to, transcending, and transforming that world because they have appropriated numerous ways of seeing it. Generally speaking, they tend to be
more resourceful and creative in the way they see and shape reality.
African Americans have had to be creative just to survive. This is not only
true materially but especially culturally and spiritually. This survival has
been aided by their ability to adapt to a variety of conditions.

African American spirituality has provided black people with the freedom and capacity to use this twoness for positive adaptation and spiritual
cohesion. The twoness of consciousness has not always led to psychological disintegration for black people but has also provided a kind of creative edge over their adversaries, which is often ignored. The ability to appropriate the implements and survival elements of the larger Anglo
culture, to look at the world and life situations through a variety of lenses,
is the result of a spirituality that implores black people to cultivate creativity as a creative response to external reality.

Freedom is thus actualized in the capacity to range or vacillate between alternative forms of consciousness and modes of being for survival. This means accommodation or revolution, adaptation or cooperation, humanization or radicalization. Because black people have been conditioned to view the world through their own as well as the white man's eyes, they have in some respects acquired more fluency and dexterity in actualizing themselves in society. This doubleness has not inevitably led to a limitation of possibilities but the establishment of alternative modes of being that have facilitated black survival. Some would argue this is more reflective of the adaptive capacities of African American spirituality than some intrinsic gift advertently bestowed by Anglo culture.

What I mean here is that the great genius of African American spirituality is not only its transcendent gifts but its syncretic-synthetic and transformative capacity, that is, its ability to appropriate the useful survival elements of Anglo culture and synthesize it with African culture into a viable paradigm of human existence. Double consciousness provides a way of responding to the world and enhances the self's creative capacities. The result is alternative and oppositional modes of being, the formation of critical consciousness, and the cultivation of a creative culture of spirituality that creates its own reality, and embraces, modifies, and transcends Anglo culture and society. To achieve this facility in a world which limited cognitive and behavioral possibilities is a remarkable feat. It is my contention that African American spirituality has had a vital role in transforming the devastations and inherent self-devaluations of double consciousness into positive and creative soul force. The manifestations of this positive reality are disclosed in all forms of African culture. Black culture becomes a positive force for transforming the negativities of double consciousness into a positive life-affirming force for African Americans. The practice of spirituality has made this possible.

We affirm that this twoness is a gift because it has not, in its inculcation, precluded black people from having a critical consciousness about whites, about themselves, or the necessities of human freedom. Nor has it blinded them to seeing the virtues of whites who have aided their struggle for freedom. Ambivalence occurs when black people fail to criticize the existing order because some white people's untruth has obscured their truth, or because their oppressor's perspectives are so valued that it causes them to inherently denigrate their own. This twoness has fostered a critical consciousness and compelled black people to envision themselves as creative extensions of their own existence, whereby they can still culturally and spiritually shape reality on their own terms.

Du Bois's problem with double consciousness is that it leads to an obfuscation of self, a devaluation and contempt for anything black or

African. Thus this twoness has led some white and black people to the conclusion that black culture, spirituality, and black life in general are intrinsically inferior to the white, which results in black self-hatred and psychological and spiritual dislocation. This bi-polar consciousness is therefore destructive because it engenders a valuation of white reality and a devaluation of black existence.

We believe the value of binary consciousness is precisely its capacity to bestow on black people different ways of seeing things. It has equally empowered them to criticize and dismantle the perspectives that are oppressive, dehumanizing, and ultimately self-annihilating. This critical consciousness is a hallmark of black culture and life because while white oppression of black people is often a topic of critical discussion among African Americans, it is not the ultimate focal point of black existence.

In other words, because one has the capacity to look at the world through white eyes does not mean that one is oblivious to white oppression. Critical consciousness through white eyes may say that black people are not free, but critical consciousness through black eyes says that white people are not free either. Is the white person who averts and avoids the black person really ontologically and racially free? He or she may be free to move about geographically, to wield political and economic power, and even to live on another planet, but is he or she truly free spiritually and ontologically? Is he free in mind, body, and soul, or does his racial phobia cause him to be a prisoner in his own flesh? There are varying degrees of freedom.

Historically speaking, black Americans may not have been socially, geographically, or politically free, but they have created a culture of freedom that allows them to use their spirituality to actualize themselves as whole human persons through creative thought and behavior. White people may be socially and politically free but may not have used their spirituality as a means of actualizing themselves as free persons in American society in the manner of black Americans for psychological, spiritual, and physical survival. Black people in America have had to use spirituality as a means of self-actualization and survival. They could not have survived without it in a world that continually tried to destroy their personhood, power, and inherent self-worth. This is the great gift of African American spirituality: how it has empowered black people to appropriate out of existential necessities a double consciousness, to establish cultural, spiritual, and ontological freedom and alternative modes of being, without losing their souls and minds in the quagmires of despair and self-destruction.

How has this double consciousness informed African American spirituality as a practice of human freedom? Since slavery black people have had four basic lenses through which to view themselves: their own, their peers', their white masters', and God's. Fortunately, their spirituality prompted them to see themselves more through God's eyes and not those of their oppressors, and this has been a liberating element of black culture and spirituality. Black people's survival was precisely tied to their capacity to replace the optic of their master with the spectacle of God, which fostered self-esteem and empowerment amid desecrating and dehumanizing conditions. Black spirituality prompted the transformation of a negative into a positive reality by taking this twoness and making it beneficial. This is an expression of freedom and also a vital element of black culture and spirituality.

In terms of critical consciousness and freedom, black people have either chosen to look at themselves through the eyes of their white slave masters and oppressors, which brings self-devaluation and contempt, or through the eyes of God, which brings affirmation and self-aggrandizement. Viewing themselves through the eyes of their masters has also created a desire to emulate certain positive aspects of Anglo culture. Black spirituality encourages black people to look at themselves through the lenses of God and not those of their oppressors. Any assessment of black life by whites is a penultimate description of the black condition and plight, not an ultimate definition of black personhood and being. The ability to take the processes of objectification and dehumanization of black personhood and transform them into a consciousness of spiritual empowerment has been a saving grace of black freedom and a hallmark of black spirituality and black culture.

Black people's capacity to create culture in response to racism and oppression is a freedom that emanates from the black culture soul and creative black soul force. When social and political freedoms were not accorded to black people, they created distinct cultural and spiritual realities that became the chief cornerstones of their psychological and spiritual survival. If slaves were not free to go where they pleased, they were spiritually free to imagine, to create an inner world both in the here and beyond. Their spirituality encouraged them to see life, however cruel, in positive ways and to create a culture of response that reinforced their sanity, identity, and integrity as spiritual beings. This gift of imagination inherent in black spiritual freedom is disclosed in every aspect of black life and culture in America.

Binary or double consciousness has inadvertently forced black people to adopt alternative and critical modes of consciousness and being, which has aided their survival and facilitated spiritual and cultural freedom.

American Constitutional Culture

Within certain sectors of black political and religious thought, it is not politically correct to reveal the foibles and problems of African Americans.

The truth is that black scholars must seriously explore the positive impact of American constitutional culture on the formation of black consciousness, culture, and spirituality. It is highly problematic that this great gift of Anglo-American experience is highly negated as a reasonable influence on our spiritual formation as African Americans.

Part of the problem may be ascribed to the desire of black scholars to retrieve their African past and to the nationalistic impulse to sever any hints of cultural ties to people of Anglo descent. This is also due to the great contradictions of American constitutional culture in that some of the original framers of the Constitution were slave holders who viewed blacks as inferior and exploited and dehumanized them for economic reasons. This is especially critical in American society where the long history of racial discrimination and oppression by whites is a significant aspect of the African American experience. Rather than embrace the cultural influences of whites who have historically oppressed blacks, it is more apropos to negate them all entirely even if that denial borders on misconstruction. It is more fitting to denounce white oppressors entirely than to claim any aspect of their culture as a positive factor in the formation of the African American experience. We curiously adopt either/or orientations despite our co-dependency as whites and blacks.

It is my belief the term "African"American signifies a confluence of the best of Africa and the European-American experiences. In other words, the formation and development of the African American experience has been impacted by blacks and whites. All too often the negative aspects of Anglo culture are accentuated in the black experience because of white racism. The genius of African American spirituality resides in its own elective affinities, the manner in which it has subtly and thoroughly appropriated, integrated, transformed, and synthesized various aspects of African and Anglo culture into a living hermeneutic of positive transformation and human survival. This is the genius of black freedom.

Accordingly, Anglo-American constitutional culture has had a strong influence on the spirituality of black people, and we might venture to say that this culture of freedom, more than "white Christianity" per se, has in many ways had an overriding impact on the development of African American freedom. Robert N. Bellah has discussed quite thoroughly the significance of American civil religion. It is precisely this "religion" that has at its core American constitutional precepts that have shaped in part notions of what is moral in the public domain.[11] It is true that the original framers of the Constitution may not have viewed black people as the beneficiaries of the new American experiment. Thus one could further argue historically that the systematic denial of certain freedoms to black Americans has been a heinous subversion of the Constitution itself. This does not, however, negate the fact that the culture of social, political, and economic freedom that distinguishes America as a unique nation has ingrained itself in the spirituality, culture, aspirations, and civic expectations of African American people. In the words of that great poet Langston Hughes, "I, Too, Sing America."[12]

American constitutional culture has invariably raised the banner of collective hope and freedom for black Americans in the social and political realms, and although black Americans know that they have been thoroughly and systematically denied various freedoms, it has not precluded their fundamental grasp of its importance for black life and the fact that they, too, as American citizens are entitled to its provisions and promises. American constitutional culture articulates the necessities of freedom in the social and political realm, and blacks have always taken this seriously. To practice freedom is to have an inward spirituality and an outward striving for it in the larger society. It is not sufficient to have inward longings for freedom. To be truly American is to live free spiritually, culturally, politically, and socially, internally as well as externally.

Thus the positive impact of American constitutional culture has shaped the actualization of black freedom in the larger culture and society. It has also, for all practical purposes, provided civic and moral foundation to black freedom in the American context. One cannot in American constitutional culture proclaim freedom for some while denying it to others. One cannot be American and remain unfree. American constitutional culture has engrafted itself into the spirituality of African Americans by establishing in the public domain the rights of all Americans to life, liberty, and the pursuit of happiness. Such rights must be realized in the social and political realms.

As stated earlier, this culture of democratic freedom has perhaps had more impact on the spirituality of African Americans than on the practice of Anglicized versions of Christianity. That is to say, this larger culture or ethos of freedom has more definitively shaped black expectations of freedom than has the white church or Christianity. While vital linkages remain between Christian belief and American constitutional culture in their mutual valuations of human freedom, the Constitution itself has been more or less the holy grail of black freedom in the corporate realm of American society.

In other words, coupled with their firm belief in God who bestows the rights of freedom to all African Americans, American constitutional culture perhaps shapes black freedom more than any other reality in Anglo-American society.

Two

The Spiritual Dynamics
of African American Freedom

In chapter 1 we explored the sources of African and African American spirituality and affirmed their importance in fathoming or informing the idea of human freedom. Now we turn our attention to the dynamics of African American spirituality and their influence on the praxis of black freedom.

African American spirituality is an expression of human freedom. It is not simply a collective social goal; it has been a process, a style of existence, a mode of consciousness and being, which has enabled black Americans to survive amid subtle and flagrant forms of racism and oppression. Black life in America has its own norms and forms, beliefs, structures, and practices that make African American life and culture a unique form of human existence.

Such realities are a synthesis of Anglo and African cultural realities and have formed themselves into an African American spirituality that impacts the consciousness, identity, aspirations, and culture of African Americans and that has been a principal catalyst in helping black people maintain spiritual vitality and social well-being despite their troubles in this land.

Our contention in this work is that African American spirituality not only shapes consciousness, beliefs, realities, and expectations of black life in America, but as ritual practice it also lends itself to the formation of a living black cultural archive and hermeneutic, which reinforces the positive values and identity formation of African American people. These functions have historical and contemporary value. They not only helped black slaves transcend the perils of slavery but continue to help black people face current adversities in the present context of the American experience.

Translation

The reality of freedom underscored in the praxis of African American spirituality is also embodied in the transformation of African American life. The fundamental purpose of black faith and belief is to change the conditions thwarting the full realization of black personhood and potential into positive reality. This means the transformation of the self and soul as well as the larger society.

We stated earlier that the creativity of black culture and black spirituality is a hallmark of African American freedom. While the harsh social conditions of slavery and discrimination could not be expediently transformed, blacks were emancipated in mind and soul through the creation of black culture and the practice of spirituality. Here blacks were free to fashion their own world as an autonomous and oppositional response to the hegemonic culture and its prevailing forms of domination.

Thus a significant aspect of African American spirituality is the manner in which it has used culture and spirituality to translate the absurdities of black existence into some viable rubric of human existence. *Translation* is the ability to create or devise a soul language, idiom, or ethos of functional and symbolic meaning and value. The task of translation is to modify existing forms of life and reality into systems of value and meaning that give power and purpose to the translator. The result is the creation of realities whose meanings and symbolism augment the struggle for personhood and survival.

African American spirituality as praxis has always worked to translate the language and symbols of white racism, oppression, and Anglo culture into systems of power and meaning for African Americans. Every major reality relegated by whites to blacks in America—from culture to community, from religion to foodways—has undergone some process of translation so as not only to create and preserve the psychological and spiritual freedom of black people but also to establish a culture of creativity and cooperation that establishes, reinforces, and transcends the sources and uniqueness of black identity and consciousness. The capacity to translate and transform reality into a meaningful culture of creativity and spirituality is a foundation of the African American paradigm of freedom. That black people have been able to achieve this under such unmitigating conditions exemplifies a power to name, define, and determine for oneself that which is vital. While some would argue that such transformation occurred out of necessity, that black people really had no choice but to do such, my contention is that their creativity in culture and spirituality not only established a unique paradigm of freedom but also preserved a measure of psychological distance and autonomy from their oppressors so they could comfortably create and construct a reality of survival.

At the heart of black spirituality then is the concept of human transformation. But transformation cannot occur without translation into new litanies of reality and being. The religious faith and belief of African Americans has always sought to change existing realities and structures into new idioms and languages of power and meaning. This is manifested in every aspect of black life, from the way blacks took the music of Europeans and transformed it into vital music of their own to the adaptation of other cultural and social realities.

The objective of translation is to create new structures of consciousness, culture, society, and belief from the hegemonic culture while preserving the integrity of one's own. This means current systems of belief and value are infused with greater power and meaning for the translator. Again, such patterns are evidenced in music—the spirituals, the blues, jazz—and the creation of black art and other media of culture. The structures of the dominant culture are thus mutated into relevant survival mechanisms for the oppressed. We might also assert that subcultures of the oppressed are also appropriated by the larger culture to further its purposes in a similar manner. The fact that black people in America have successfully adopted and adapted the structures of the larger culture for their own purposes exemplifies a freedom and propensity to be life-transforming and self-determining persons. Contrary to popular opinion, slavery and racism did not rob African Americans of the capacity to think and create, to forge the absurdities of their existence into dynamic life fulfilling possibilities.

Translation also presupposes existing systems of value and meaning into which the adapted reality is conformed and altered. It is generally assumed in analyses of the black life and white culture that the former had to insinuate itself into the latter to create meaningful patterns of survival. While this may be true, it is equally feasible that existing structures of Anglo culture were modified to fit those structures of African consciousness and culture that black people already possessed.

The truth is that the African American paradigm of human freedom culminates in the way African Americans have translated existing cultural structures into viable patterns of existence while simultaneously establishing and perpetuating their own identity and freedom.

In other words, black culture and spirituality did not form simply because white folks rebuked and segregated black people, thus compelling them to construct their own reality by default. They were created primarily out of the powers of creativity and invention that prompted African Americans to seize and possess the invaluable aspects of the larger culture for survival and wed them with their own. Creative soul force compelled black Americans to creatively produce their own culture for survival.

This self-initiative and entrepreneurial impulse was congenitally instilled through the practice of spirituality and is a vital implement of cultural and social transformation. The perpetual task of practitioners of black spirituality is to transform those systems and cultures of racism, dehumanization, self-hatred, and devaluation into positive self-identity, humanization for the revaluation and empowerment of black life. Transformation is essential to the African American paradigm of freedom, for black people have always seen the need to take reality and shape it into something for meaningful survival.

The theology of African American spirituality then does not encourage blacks to be the passive recipients of reality, to take whatever is dealt them without resistance or defiance, but to seize the discord of their social plight and translate it into litanies of positive soul survival. God intends for the oppressed to seize the day in order to transform the terrors of their condition into something positive and glorious that augments their practice of human freedom.

Liberation

Translation means not only transformation but liberation. *Liberation* is the progressive manumission from a condition of bondage to a condition of freedom. It means breaking free from the constraints of servitude and subjugation. Liberation is practiced in the social realm through the toppling of tyrannies and in the personal realm in the creation and perpetuation of black culture and spirituality as a creative and resistant soul force response to oppression.

Analyses of black freedom in America tend largely to use Anglo sociopolitical presuppositions as an index to how free African Americans really are in relation to the powers. Invariably all discussions regarding black freedom in America focus on emancipation from external, political, and social power structures. Seldom does analysis underscore models of internal, spiritual, and psychological freedom that prevent complete enslavement and domestication of black people by whites. It is precisely this emphasis on the internal spiritual aspects of liberation through the practice of spirituality and the creation of black culture that makes the African American paradigm of freedom unique.[1] But the African American paradigm does not simply embrace external liberation from oppressive structures in society. It includes the emancipation of mind, soul, and spirit from psychological, spiritual, and cultural tyrannies from within a dominant society. Liberation, therefore, is an interior affair of the mind and spirit as well as an external venture of the body and soul from physical bondage.

African American spirituality then has been instrumental in giving black people the spiritual and cultural elements to liberate themselves from those internal tyrannies that sequester the soul and destroy the mind. Black freedom means having the ability to think spiritually and create culturally, to resist all forms of domestication and dehumanization that destroy the capacity for black self-determination.

Since its inception, African American spirituality has specialized in instilling in black people those strategies, behaviors, beliefs, and values that thwart their complete psychological and spiritual decimation. Such spiritual practice has equipped black people with the capacity to free themselves from those realities and beliefs that impair their social and spiritual progress.

Psychological and relational transformation are also important features of African American spirituality. Psychological transformation has helped blacks psychically adjust, confront, and surmount the perils of servitude. The liturgical forms of African American spirituality have helped create an ethos that enables blacks to evade complete psychic devastation by racism and oppression.

The brutality and inhumanity perpetrated against African Americans throughout their history in America from slavery, in which the black family was virtually destroyed, to lynchings, physical castration, segregation, and Jim Crow have all had an adverse psychological impact on African Americans, particularly black men. The negative affects of such atrocities could have been far greater had not African American spirituality operated as a humanizing, consolidating, and consoling force for black Americans. The prayers, preaching, and liturgies of spirituality from the hush harbor meetings of early slave religion to the black church have all worked to prevent the psychic obliteration of African Americans. Equally significant in preventing such annihilation is the creation of black culture as expressed through music, folk tales, humor, and other idioms of culture, which reinforced their sanity and personhood.

Relational transformation is important because it signifies the capacity of African Americans to use their spirituality as a catalyst for the formation of meaningful and viable relationships, which ultimately insulate them from complete psychic and spiritual annihilation. The practice of spirituality in camp meetings and other forums created a context for the formation of vital relationships in human community. The fact that blacks could come together to create rituals of freedom through preaching, prayer, healing, music, and other idioms exemplified an ability to maintain a relational matrix of unity within the larger community. When blacks had been demoralized by their oppressors, the establishment of meaningful relationships provided a foundation for personal healing and empowerment. As one man observed, "I might be a nigger in the white man's eyes, but in the eyes of my children, church, and community I am a man." The practice of black spirituality created an arena where black relationships could be established, solidified, and perpetuated, undergirded by religious symbols, signs, and practices that would become the ultimate guideposts to black life in America. The key here is transformation, the ways in which black faith and belief have transformed the harsh conditions of slavery, racism, and oppression into positive and creative black life forces.

Transformation means that God is still in charge of creation, that God makes a way out of no way, that the outsiders will be transformed into insiders, and the oppressed will be set free. Because God specializes in changing the conditions of African Americans into a positive reality, African American spiritual praxis has succeeded in promulgating and instilling in them this important belief. God will transform the lives of the oppressed and the oppressed will transform their peculiar condition into a meaningful litany of praise and thanksgiving for human empowerment and existence.

Because the establishment of psychic wholeness and well-being through the cultivation of positive relationships is so important in African American life, the practice of spirituality as a vehicle of personal and communal transformation has provided African Americans with the means of surviving the troubles of their American experience.

Thus the language of oppression is translated into the language of freedom. The reality of repression and discrimination is transformed into a culture of creativity that inherently defies and resists all attempts at complete subjugation, domestication, and devaluation. African American spirituality as a practice of freedom has thus enabled black Americans to become not only the recipients but also the agents of divine transformation through various processes of cultural and spiritual liberation.

Consecration

It is not unusual for the victims of prolonged and systemic racism and oppression to profane and desacralize the value and worth of their own lives. The abomination of racism and various forms of oppression resides in the myriad ways the lives of the oppressed are stripped of any sanctity and value in the eyes of their oppressors, themselves, and other human beings. The final mark of a people's complete enslavement can be measured in terms of the ways in which they have allowed their conquerors to destroy their sense of the personal sanctity and self-worth.

It is my contention and a principal premise of this project that African American spiritual praxis has precluded the desacralization of black life and thus thwarted the complete, unmitigated desecration of African American people. Put simply, black people's belief in God and their unwavering practice of sound spiritual precepts have prevented their adversaries from decimating their sense of the sanctity of life.

Reading the history of African Americans, one discovers that numerous whites had a largely brutal disregard for black life from the beginning of

American slavery. Contrary to revisionist thinkers who seek to take the sting out of American slavery and white racism by humanizing all white masters, overseers, and their overlords, history reveals a long litany of brutality and cruelty by whites toward blacks. Slave narratives and the chronicles of black America are replete with stories of black women who were raped, black children beaten and ripped from their families, and black men and boys beaten into sniveling and fawning submission by white masters. The cruelties, though less flagrant, continue today in black communities where black men are criminalized, terrorized by the Ku Klux Klan, brutalized by white police officers, and thrown into prison. The experiences of Emmett Till and Rodney King are just two examples of modern brutality against blacks.

The history of black Americans is the story of a people subject to terror, racism, and unmitigated oppression and murder in a racist society. The fact that this kind of treatment could happen to a people means that black life has largely been profaned and dehumanized in the eyes of some whites and even blacks in American society.

A further tragedy is how blacks have assailed and assaulted each other, thus further denegrating the sanctity of black life. We see this through black-on-black crime, and the various forms of dehumanization that blacks commit against each other.

The role of African American spirituality has been the restoration of the sacredness of black life amid the desacralizing forces of American society. While white racism, brutality, and oppression have historically created the conditions for the desecration of black life, the practice of black spirituality has conversely consecrated and restored black self-worth through various ritual practices and a firm belief in God.

Mercy

African Americans have, thus, always relied on a thoroughgoing belief in a God of sanctity, mercy, and transformation. In fact, it has been precisely the process of mercy in relation to both themselves and their oppressors that the sacredness of black life has taken on greater value and meaning. Firm belief in God has led to the practice of mercy by African Americans in relation to white racists, for there have been countless times in their experience with whites where physical retaliation and annihilation of white racist tormentors and lynchers would have been perfectly warranted but was summarily withheld because of belief in the sacredness of life itself.

The praxis of African American spirituality affirms the sanctity of all life, even those of slavers and racists; otherwise a much more brutal history between the races could have transpired. I have termed this *mercification*, which is the practice of grace and mercy in the midst of dehumanization and personal desecration. This means that however much a person becomes an adversary, that person shall never lose the sacred status of person, for the practice of mercy not only preserves the sacredness of persons, both oppressors and oppressed, but also the autonomy of the Creator who created them as persons.

Nonviolence

Howard Thurman observes: "The awareness that a man is a child of God of religion, who is at one and the same time the God of life, creates a profound faith in life that nothing can destroy."[2] Nonviolence, the freedom not to destroy another life because of self-sanctity and the sacredness of life, is a very important aspect of African American spiritual freedom.

Many have argued that black religion and spirituality have largely been pacifying, accommodationist forces that have coerced African Americans into acquiescing to the brutality of their oppressors. They contend that black religion has made cowards of the masses of blacks because of white Christian brainwashing. Black faith and belief, they also argue, have instilled too much reverence and fear of the whites and thus made blacks co-conspirators in their own subjugation.

While there may be some truth in all this, I believe that because blacks still view themselves as sacred persons of infinite worth and life as sacred, they are able to draw on spiritual powers and resources that have prevented their complete consumption by venomous hatred and the ventilation of violence toward all white people. Because black people still affirm self-sanctity and worth despite the terrors and cruelties of racism, they are able to extend that belief even to their enemies. Again, Howard Thurman is helpful:

> A man's conviction that he is God's child automatically tends to shift the basis of his relationship with all his fellows. He recognizes at once that to fear a man, whatever may be that man's power over him, is a basic denial of the integrity of his very life. It lifts that mere man to a place of preeminence that belongs to God and to God alone. He who fears is literally delivered to destruction.[3]

Contrary to the idea that such behavior signifies that blacks advertently complied with their own psychological and spiritual slavery, the fact that blacks were able to withstand the consuming forces of racial hatred and annihilation suggests they were able to maintain a measure of personal freedom and autonomy that preserved their own self-worth and sanctity. Had blacks used more violent means of gaining their freedom by trying to destroy all the whites who enslaved and oppressed them, it would have meant the loss of personal sanctification and the enthronement of fear as a guiding force in their lives. It would also have meant the loss of a certain moral authority in God's eyes and their own.

This view is especially important given the hegemony and authority of God in the lives of black people and the fact that God would ultimately liberate them from their oppressors. For some, this analysis may seem curious, but showing mercy by withholding the violent and brutal destruction of whites helped maintain black humanity and sacredness in the midst of perpetually profane and violent circumstances.

Freedom not only means having the courage to strike a physical blow for liberation through violence, as in the case of Nat Turner and others, but may equally mean having the courage and humanity not to strike a blow that will destroy the life of another. This is a special kind of freedom, strength, and fearlessness. We saw this freedom and strength exemplified in the Civil Rights movement, where blacks took blows from their adversaries without striking back. Because African American spirituality has instilled in blacks a sense of dignity and somebodiness, they have largely, through the practice of mercy and grace, overcome the temptation to use violence as the only answer to racism and oppression. Resistance is, therefore, not only subverting tyrannical and oppressive powers but having the moral capacity and temerity to withhold violent retribution toward enemies even when such action may be perfectly justified.

In order for such resistance to occur on such a wide scale, black people had to believe in the sanctity of life. Slavery, for all practical purposes, could have been terminated by the cooks on the plantation who served their masters' food. Were there not a reverence for the sanctity of life, black cooks on white plantations could have cruelly poisoned their masters and families. But because the practice of spirituality emphasized the sanctity of life, blacks largely refrained from such genocidally destructive acts although some believe it would have been a pertinent rejoinder to the atrocities of slavery.

Perhaps no other persons besides Native Americans have been as desecrated, vilified, and dehumanized as African Americans, but the practice of spirituality and faith has remarkably prevented them from harboring a lingering hatred for their tormentors. This resiliency and capacity to overcome the cruelties of life is intimately bound to the sanctity of life, a firm belief that God, others, and all of creation are sacred and that no one has the right to take the life of another because God will ultimately correct all wrongs. This view is also inherent in African creation cosmology and extends into African American spirituality. All life is sacred, and only God can ultimately make final judgments on the worth and value of human life. Love of self and God are strong deterrents to self-annihilating behavior.

The practice of grace and mercy of blacks toward whites has not simply occurred because there have always been good white Christian people who graciously came to their aid but because the practice of faith warranted it and the creation of black culture as a praxis of freedom became an instrument that diffused and sublimated black anger and hatred into a powerful expression of creativity and survival. Napoleon Bonaparte once observed that religion kept the poor from killing the rich. The spirituality of African Americans has largely prevented blacks from killing both whites and themselves in response to the malignities of their condition.

Through the creation of culture and the practice of spirituality, African Americans have avoided the paths of destruction that could have been easily charted under such inhumane conditions. Thus culture has had a consecrating function insofar as it allowed black people to create alternative idioms and avenues of expression that would bring both solace and relief to their existential despair.

Again it was not fear of white people or fear of death that prevented blacks from desecrating life but firm belief in personal sanctity and the consecrating power of God. This means that African American spirituality has invariably taught black people that since they are of ultimate value in God's eyes, they should have a supreme reverence for themselves. The more white people tried to destroy their sense of personal sanctity, the more their faith and belief resisted such denigration. Regarding human hatred, Thurman observes:

> It is this kind of attitude that is developed in the mind and souls of the weak and the disinherited. As they look out upon their world, they recognize at once that they are the victims of a systematic denial of the rights and privileges that are theirs, by virtue both of their being human and of their citizenship. . . . Because they are despised, they despise themselves. If they reject the judgment, hatred may serve as a device for rebuilding, step by perilous step, the foundation for individual significance; so that from within the intensity of their necessity they declare their right to exist, despite the judgment of the environment.[4]

The transcendent value of consecration cannot be obviated, for in viewing the black self as ultimately a sacred self, black people overcame their human predicament. There is no other force in African American life and thought having the power and capacity to shape black thinking and behavior as spirituality and the black church. Spirituality is the one sovereign area of black existence that has resisted all attempts by whites and the larger culture to define and domesticate it into complete meaninglessness.

The preservation of the sacred, then, in black life has helped African Americans to overcome complete annihilation by whites and others in this society. It has instilled in them a fearlessness and created a personal soul force that has yet to be destroyed. African American spirituality is the only force that can claim such supremacy in getting black people over the pain of living in America. Pure soul force has prevented blacks from falling into the quagmires of despair and desolation. Because the practice of black spirituality has emphasized the cultivation of resistant and creative soul force, blacks have avoided the psychological depression and dementia so characteristic of oppressed peoples.

The black self is a sacred self and soul force is a sanctifying, unifying reality for black life in America. Because of the consecrating value of African American spirituality, black people have created idioms and ethos of thinking and being that have helped them maintain their humanity, dignity, and sanity. Embracing personal sanctification has helped African Americans to sidestep much of the violent destruction that characterizes their mistreatment in America.

The question is how can a people subject to the terror and violence of African Americans not become equally violent in relation to their perpetrators? In other words, how could black people have largely avoided the widespread and wholesale retribution of violence against some whites who have mercilessly and consistently used violence against them? The humanizing and consecrating aspects of African American spirituality have largely dispelled such antagonistic methods of retaliation. This does not mean that black people are not violent or have not used violence against whites or themselves in this society. It only means that, given the magnitude and nature of violence used on them, they have not used violence as a principal recourse to the violence of white racism and oppression.

In speaking of violence we are not simply addressing the physical type but also what Robert McAfee Brown describes as *structural violence*.[5] This form of violence includes psychological, emotional, and relational violence, violence that slowly destroys a person's self-esteem, value, and self-worth. Poverty is a form of structural violence, for while it is not as overt as physical violence, its devastation is just as ominous.

African Americans have been systematically and abundantly subjected to physical and structural violence. The violence of slavery and racism is not only embodied in physical brutalities but psychological and relational dismemberment wherein the oppressed are thoroughly denied the amenities and basic comforts accorded fully to human beings. Manifestations of such violence are disseminated in the larger culture through the media and the general specter of fear and suspicion fomented around black people, particularly black males.

This is violence of the worst type because it not only denigrates the individual but creates an aura of fear and hatred for the person that inherently justifies his or her annihilation. For example, I have always wondered why in America the predominant image of fear and violence is the

African American male. While some of this fear may be justified, much of it cannot. How is it that in the history of violence in Western civilization black males have had only a minuscule role, yet they are depicted as the predominant perpetrators of violence in America? These stereotypes are promulgated in the media as emblematic of black males as a whole when in truth they symbolize a minority of black men. Most African American males are law-abiding, nonviolent citizens. They obey the law and respect the rights of others.

Here we essentially have various processes of dehumanization and desecration subtly created by casting black males as the preponderant instigators of violence in America. A result of such desecration is that black males are virtually viewed as brutal, uncaring, and less than human, persons to be feared, avoided, and even destroyed by any means. The idea that black males are endangered is not unfounded.

Transformative Sacredness

African American spirituality and the black church have always preserved the sanctity of black life and the important role of black men and women in shaping the destiny of their families and communities. More than any other institution in black society, the precepts and beliefs of African American spiritual praxis has consecrated the meaning and value of black life in African American communities.

By viewing themselves as sacred persons, as God's anointed children, black people used spirituality as the basis for defining their true personhood against the dehumanization of white racism. While racism described a condition of black people, spirituality helped define the worth of black power and potentiality as a means of venerating black existence.

We must remember that the consecrating dimensions of black spirituality in relation to black life do not advocate a passive acquiescence to white dehumanization but the development of psychological, physical, cultural, and spiritual resources that give them the upper hand in a no-win situation. For example, by viewing themselves as sacred, blacks were still able to harness those supernatural and natural resources and energies oblivious to their oppressors that would give them the strength and courage to succeed and overcome their condition. By calling on God and centering their lives and belief in God, they were invariably open to a word from on high that would empower them to deal with the troubles they encountered in their daily struggle for love, truth, and justice.

Cultivating the sacred self means developing those spiritual and ethereal resources that continually connect black people with divine reality. This means that black life and culture are replete with beliefs and references to the divine. Thus the language and behavior of black people consistently exemplify references to God and divine order so that the sacred self can always be affirmed amid desacralizing and dehumanizing circumstances. The sacred self's affirmation of this mode of consciousness and existence is its way of breaking through those barriers and impediments that seek to bind and enslave it. The more I affirm my "God self," the less I confirm the capacity of others to enslave and dehumanize those aspects of myself that they rationalize as a basis for my personal denigration.

Thus the value of consecration is not only its power to instill within the black oppressed a sense of their own self-sanctity but the formation of an ethos of being and consciousness that uses divine reality as the ultimate ground and reference point for black behavior and belief. Blacks are then able to survive the cruelties of slavery and racism because in their practice of the sacred self, they transcend the absurdities of their human condition.

Small wonder why the language, thought, actions, and beliefs of black people are replete with references to God and divine reality. Statements such as "Don't worry about it because the Lord will take care of it," "Trust in the Lord," and "God is good" are just small examples of the practice of this sacred self by African Americans.

Nothing is done or conceived without giving God praise and adulation, and this simple daily practice of spirituality has been a primary source of spiritual empowerment and freedom for black people in America for hundreds of years. The fact that blacks have been able to affirm and practice a sacred self in the midst of the desecrating and dehumanizing realities of the American experience attests to the majesty and power of God both to consecrate and liberate the oppressed from the profanities of dehumanization.

The fact that black people do not hate all white people after all that has been done to them affirms the power of the sacred as an operational force in black life. It means that God, through mercy, consecration, and grace, has bestowed on African Americans the ability to transform and transcend their human predicament. It also suggests that a kind of "freedom from" is established in response to the violation of one's person, a freedom from hatred, self-deprecation, and violent self-destruction at the provocations of white racism.

Howard Thurman again observes:

> A man knows precisely what he can do to you or what epithet he can hurl against you in order to make you lose your temper, your equilibrium, then he can always keep you under subjection. It is man's reaction to things that determines their ability to exercise power over him.[6]

By not reacting to the provocations of adversaries, blacks have been able to establish a sense of personal autonomy and self-control under incendiary conditions. This freedom characterizes the African American experience. By practicing faith and possessing a sense of the self as a sacred entity, black people have largely established an idiom of self-dignity and control that ultimately cannot be determined by their adversaries. The capacity not to allow their adversaries to control their response to the conditions of oppression is a freedom seldom delineated.

Again, many critics argue that black religion and spirituality have instilled fear of whites within blacks. The issue here is not having the freedom to control one's response but that white people have instilled so much fear in black people that they are too afraid to do otherwise for fear of punishment or death. It is my contention that freedom from such violent and denigrating responses to white brutality and racism exemplifies a self-control rooted in personal sanctity and autonomy. By knowing that I am a child of God, a person of worth and dignity by virtue of my practice of spirituality, there is nothing my adversaries can do to instill fear and intimidation in me as a person. There is nothing they can do so as to bring me so low as to hate myself or them. Hatred is nonfreedom, a form of psychological and spiritual slavery. This means that I am not afraid to die nor afraid to resist employing those harsher methods of rebellion that would be justified by the realities of oppression.

African American spirituality has thus instilled in blacks a personal dignity and autonomy, sanctity, and self-worth whose response to oppression cannot be ultimately determined by white racists or other adversaries because it means living fearlessly and having a sense of unwavering personal strength in relation to one's enemies. This practice of nonviolence and personal freedom have long been a hallmark of African American spirituality.

Choosing nonviolence as opposed to violence as a predominant mode of response to oppressors and racists has not transpired because black people have been taught to be cowards by their faith but because they have always had a deeper sense of personal sanctity and worth. The practice of spirituality has always encouraged the cultivation of those resources and modalities that would morally elevate them above their adversaries. This means that black people would always create culture in response to oppression as an expression of freedom and autonomy or cultivate other modes of spiritual behavior and belief that would enable them to confront and transcend the perils of their condition.

Spirituality as a consecrating force for change in black life means responding to life on one's own terms and creating a consciousness and culture that refutes and negates the dehumanizing and denigrating aspects of white racism and oppression.

Three

Living Freely and Spiritually

We have stated thus far that a benchmark of the African American paradigm of freedom is the way in which culture and spirituality create a basis for the creative and transcendent expression of black life and belief. The task for African Americans has always been to exceed the constraints and disaffections externally imposed upon them by racist behavior and thinking. Going beyond the debilitating strictures of white racism has meant creating a place for the black self to go beyond itself in a world that would not let it be itself. This has meant the creative construction of other selves, realities, and idioms of black behavior and belief that debunk and deprecate all attempts by adversaries to devalue and desecrate black life. Herein lies the practice of African American freedom as a unique entity. The spirituality and culture of African Americans have preserved a freedom, creativity, and autonomy of being in a world that has fervently tried to name, reduce, define, and seduce that being into a permanently dehumanized existence.

Dona Richards is again helpful in her analysis of African American spirituality:

> Out of nothingness we built a world. In an environment which denied black being, we insisted on being. Oppressed by dehumanizing circumstance we still found something in which to recognize enough of ourselves to revitalize our souls—to create new selves. From the very first we gave expression to the divine in us for it was our humanity. It was out of this expression of divinity that a reformulated, African-derived cultural expression was to emerge, a cultural expression peculiar to the North American circumstance, of necessity influenced by Europe, influenced by the harshness and paternalism of the slave condition, influenced even by the denigration of the African heritage. The expressions which emerged were our language, our music, our dance, our thought patterns, our laughter, our walk, our spirituality. These

were the vehicles through which the African ethos expressed itself in America.[1]

African American spirituality has prevented blacks from accepting dehumanization as a determinant for defining black personhood and humanity and has helped them develop mechanisms of survival that unequivocally refute the practice of recrimination as a legitimate form of retaliation to whites. Dona Richards says that, "to survive as Africans, to survive spiritually, we had to create meaning. We had to re-create order in the midst of chaos."[2] In others, not only would blacks not accept the definitions, denigrations, and devaluations perpetrated against them by adversaries as a means of reducing their self-worth but would equally renounce the cruel methods of white dehumanization as a legitimate means to redress their condition. This means that black people neither ultimately accepted the grounds or rationale of white racism and oppression nor endorsed the means of white subjugation of black people as a foundation for winning their own social and political freedom. The fact that black people could fashion and choose the terms of moral response to their oppression is a freedom often taken for granted. Their ability to choose the terms of their response exemplifies a unique spiritual and moral freedom.

Because much analyses of black freedom focuses only on the external social and political types, the value of the African American paradigm in helping back people to cultivate an inner strength and resistance to dehumanization and oppression is often negated. That blacks have come through their American experience believing in God and practicing God's presence while simultaneously maintaining integrity, dignity, and humanity suggests a freedom of mind, body, spirit, and soul not determined by the machinations of their adversaries. This form of freedom, while primarily internal, where the mind, body, heart, and soul resist all attempts at dehumanization and domestication, is also external. African American spirituality has enabled black people to develop and sustain this inner strength and freedom against all odds. One area where this is evidenced is ontology.

Ontology is the study of the science of being. The primary foundation of white racism is ontological, for it is the systematic discrimination and oppression of a people on the basis of race. Webster's *New Universal Unabridged Dictionary* defines racism as "the program or practice of racial discrimination, segregation, persecution and domination based on racialism." *Race* is thus an ontological category having to do with the physiognomy or the countenance of human beings.

Accordingly, racism has profound theological implications as it relates to ontology, for it is difficult to condemn the created on the basis of race without condemning the Creator God who brought the various races into existence. The fact that God created different races of people confirms the capacity of God's creative imagination. Racism therefore is intrinsically antitheological and antiontological, and African American spirituality has helped black people embrace blackness as a created reality and thereby overcome the constraints created by racial ontology.

We must keep in mind that because black people are persecuted because of the color of their skin, the attainment of external freedom has been virtually impossible in American society. Black people have not been free to go where they pleased nor could they escape the stigma of blackness so ingrained in the culture and consciousness of white Americans. Blacks could not change their skin color and were thereby confined and contained on the basis of their racial ontology. Black skin thus became a mark of denigration and dishonor. The possibilities of escape to freedom socially and geographically were virtually impossible because of the obvious external marks of identification.

Because black social and political enslavement were externally imposed on the basis of skin color, black people had to develop internal modes of being and response that repudiated the various symbols, codes, and conventions externally imposed by a white racist society. These are the ontological forms of black freedom that relate to black ways of seeing, acting, thinking, and expressing black life in a white world. These ontological forms of black life and culture are largely antithetical and oppositional to the thinking, behavior, and beliefs promulgated by the dominant white culture. Let us examine these various ontological modes of human freedom.

Living the Truth of Black Existence

Black people have always had to face the hard facts and truth about American racism. The truth is that many whites hated and discriminated against black people on the basis of race. This is a central truth of American society and although racism has waned in some sectors of society, its indelible imprint on the culture and mind of people in America is still a sad and painful reality. Not all white people are racists. Many of them have denounced racism in belief and practice. However, numerous whites are the beneficiaries of racism and often find it difficult to morally extirpate it because it is so deeply woven within the matrix of American society.

Racism is perpetrated against blacks because of the color of their skin and while other reasons for racism have been delineated, from economics to fear of miscegenation, the fact remains that some white people do not like black people primarily because of their race. The same can be said of some blacks. Black skin then becomes an ontological category signifying evil and all that is bad and symbolizes categorically certain devaluational processes. The problem is not only discrimination based on race but the insidious development and practice of those attitudes, behaviors, values, and beliefs that categorically and inherently disqualify and devalue all black people. This truth has helped shape the consciousness and sensibilities of black people in America and conditioned their response to racism in America.

Accepting the truth of one's condition means that both truth and the nascent condition in which one finds oneself can be used as instruments for freeing the mind and spirit from the constraints of racism itself. By affirming the truth of their existence, blacks have been able to break and dispel much of the untruth and propaganda used to enslave and dominate them.

Accordingly, African American spirituality has not simply prepared black people for life in the other world but has helped them truthfully to face the reality of life in this world. This truth is foundational to the premise and practice of African American spirituality and the basis for black life and being in America.

The fact that God is, that God takes care of God's own, that justice and freedom will be realized by the oppressed, and things will get better in the by and by is an unequivocal affirmation of spiritual and existential truth. God is still in charge and black people still remain black, but truth will shatter the pretense, folly, and ignorance created by racism, untruth, and dehumanization.

Thus the first axiom of the ontological forms of African American spirituality as a praxis of human freedom is the affirmation, acceptance, and practice of the truth of one's existence. From the beginning black people have confronted the truths and untruths of white racism and oppression, and have spent their lives refuting those realities through the practice of spiritual and ontological truth. I am what I am, and we are what we are. Affirming the truth of one's existence creates a freedom of the self that surpasses the superficial constraints created by the realities and mythologies of racial oppression in American society.

"Walking a Different Talk"

In the previous chapter we spoke of how translation helps black people develop a new language of being in America. The ontological forms of black freedom precisely mean walking and existing in different languages and idioms of reality that are in direct cultural opposition to the

domesticating and subjugating influences of white society. The language of
spirituality has thus created within black people a unique pattern of existence whereby the thoughts, feelings, trajectories, and textures of interpretation and expression are developed in different modalities. Rather than think
in prose, black people have expressed themselves in poetry, that is to say,
rhythmically or nonrhythmically, particularly if rhythm is what is expected
by whites, or in off-beat, half-metered flirtations and reverberations. The
language of black culture and spirituality has instilled within black people
a capacity to think and shape harmony out of dissonance, concord out of
discord. The key here is the creation of those ontological modes of seeing
and being that establish their own litanies and archives of black value, legitimacy, and power. Geneva Smitherman reminds us, "In any culture, of
course, language is a tool for ordering the chaos of human experience."[3]

"Walking a different talk" means that the temperance and rhythms of
black existence in America create their own ontological and liturgical
forms of existence where up is down and down is up. It means shifting the
axis of definition of what it means to be legitimately in a white world and
defining for oneself the nature, form, and color of that existence vis-à-vis
the larger society. Creating idioms and ethos of cultural and ontological
opposition is manifested in every aspect of black life in America, and
walking a different talk epitomizes this capacity.

Blacks, therefore, may comport themselves in blues forms and variations, think and act in jazz, and not in the polite, conventional behavioral
modalities of white society and Western culture. This means that the
white "yes" will be the black "yeah" and the white "Can you believe it?"
will become the black "Can you dig it?" The point is to express one's being in a language and signature uniquely black.

"Acting black" means emulating an ontological form of reality that
uses soul force as a creative expression for being. It is precisely a characteristic of black freedom that African Americans have been able to create
this unique ethos of authentic expression in a society that has despised
and denigrated blackness both as symbol and reality. The fact that black
people can ostensibly and comfortably refer to a *black* culture, a *black* style
of being and mode of consciousness is the creative and spiritual work of
a free people who have found a comfort in being black in a society that has
used that blackness as a basis for their separation and dehumanization.

The paradox is that whites who have created the mythologies and
specter of race in America seem less comfortable in being white or ex-
trinsically referring to things white, than blacks in being black. The point
here, without oversimplifying, is that the practice of spirituality as an expression of freedom has created a context in which African Americans can
securely be who they are as ontological entities because they have estab-

lished a whole welter and culture of black beingness that creates and contains its own language, codes, and legitimacies of human existence. This language of existence has instilled within black Americans a consciousness of culture and a culture of consciousness that has at its core the practice of spirituality. For to "be" in black life is to be centered and spiritual through creative and resistant soul force. Blackness is synonymous with being spiritual and the capacity to walk and talk in a very unique language than those in power.

"Walking black" means existing in patterns and configurations that shape and sustain consciousness, identity, and spiritual vitality. The point here is that African American culture and spirituality have created an ethos or world in which the salient characteristics and modalities of black life have shaped their own consciousness and being unique to the African American. The fact that this reality of black life has been created attests to the power of African American spirituality as a life-creating and life-sustaining force for African Americans.

Moreover, this culture or ethos did not simply arise because black people were largely segregated or isolated from white people but because black spirituality and culture provided both a text and context for the wholesome emergence of an authentically black ontology that would both distinguish itself from as well as embrace and transcend other ontological forms. To achieve this without losing soul and sanity is a manifestation of a people's capacity to freely conceive, establish, name, and define reality on their own terms.

If there is such a thing as a black way of being, seeing, and acting in the world, we mean this positively and not negatively, for too often such behavior patterns have been denigrated as inferior, uncouth, or below the norms of white society. Statements such as "There you go, acting black again," or "Don't be coming at me with all that black stuff" are means of devaluing the power and worth of these behavioral modalities. To "act black" means to act with dignity and integrity, to be fully spiritual and expressive, and to establish psychological location in a society that has attempted to dislocate and dislodge it. These applications are relevant to any people notwithstanding race and culture who find themselves in similar circumstances.

The ontological power of African American spirituality as a model of freedom lies precisely in its creation of this culture of being or being of culture wherein black people can be comfortable in being who they are without getting permission from or apologizing to others for being what God authentically created them to be.

Being black and the emergence of blackness as a unique ontological category of existence in a white racist society is the ultimate expression of African American freedom. Just being comfortable in being black without second thoughts or shame in a society that has done everything possible to eradicate, destroy, or stymie such presence is a manifestation of black freedom.

The ontological forms of freedom then do not simply mean that blacks only agitate for political, social, or economic power but that they walk a different language or that they are just comfortable being the black person God created. This means that African Americans are secure in their bodies as spiritual persons, that being black is a beautiful expression of freedom and power in a society that has systematically tried to destroy the value of that identity and self-worth in all aspects. To feel securely, to think and act as a black person is to practice ontological freedom, which is simply freedom to be who one is forthrightly and unabashedly. To simply be and be black is a testimony to the power of God to uplift and sustain black people in a racist society.

However, being black does not signify hostility, anger, hatred, and rage toward white people as the predominant modalities of being although such indignation is sometimes righteously manifested, but it means to live as a creative and resistant soul force capable of adopting and adapting the circumstances of its existence in its own language, by its own powers, and under its own terms. It means living in perennial opposition to those tyrannical forms of life in whatever ways they manifest themselves that repress and stymie people's capacity to realize themselves and actualize their greatest potential as human beings of infinite worth. It is living with confidence that God is within and works through human beings, converting everything into a force for divine good.

We are not suggesting that being black does not have its foibles or contradictions as do other forms of ontology that are truly human. Black people are not perfect nor should they romanticize or sanitize their faults compared to those of others. It simply means that, contrary to popular belief, such problems are not the predominant realities shaping the consciousness and behavior of African Americans. African Americans are not primarily shaped by their problems nor do those difficulties define their humanity. The fundamental influence is a soul force spirituality that shapes order out of chaos and disillusionment. Even racism in all its formidable forms is not the only reality shaping the culture, character, and ethos of African American people.

We must remember that racism in American society embodies and signifies a whole constellation of attitudes, values, beliefs, and practices that stifle human potential. It is an anthropological flaw. The fact that some white people have been the primary adversaries of black people in America does not mean that all whites hate all blacks or vice versa. It only means that those attitudes, presuppositions, and evils created and perpetrated by whites or other peoples under the rubric of race, preventing the full realization of black personhood and the development of black potential, are thoroughly rejected and repudiated by African Americans. It also signifies that black people are largely in opposition to those despotic ontological practices of whites and other races that sanction only certain forms of beingness and culture as legitimate and valued expressions of human existence.

The problem of black freedom then is also ontological because those having the power to define and shape behavior also construct configurations of beingness that reinforce the power and dominance of a particular group. Those behaving or expressing themselves beyond the veil of the cultural and behavioral norms are thus delegitimized and denigrated. Their ontology as full persons is invalidated by the dominant culture.

African American spirituality has enabled black people to establish their own viable and legitimate ontology and black ways of being in American society by creating unique idioms of expression and being that have reinforced personal values and vitality. This African American ontology is highly opposed to those patterns of being and behavior employed by whites to delegitimize black people, thus boasting their position of dominance over them.

For example, an ontological or behavioral modality forced by whites on blacks is the idea that black people should be seen and not heard. This practice was reinforced in slavery when blacks were punished for speaking their minds and learning to read and write. The masters understood that literacy was a form of self-determination and the key to liberation resided in the power of personal expression. *Personal expression* is the ability to articulate thoughts, feelings, and aspirations through personality. *Articulation* means the capacity to name, value, and define reality. All of this relates to walking a different talk, of orienting to reality in accordance with a black way of seeing things.

Conversely, African American spirituality encourages blacks to freely express themselves in worship and in other areas of their lives. Free expression is a high prize of realizing human potential in a world that destroyed and persecuted blacks for such self-expression. In a society where just looking at a white woman too long meant death by an enraged and demented mob, black people learned to repress vital aspects of their being and personhood. Thus developing the freedom to express oneself freely and openly became a value, instilled through the practice of African American spirituality, that is in direct antithesis to the repression and silence enforced by whites. This free, creative expression is the seedbed of African American cultural freedom. Such freedom culminated in various forms of cultural and spiritual protest that manifested themselves in modalities of being that encouraged the free, unbridled expression of the creative spirit-soul of black people. Spirituality thus created avenues of freedom wherein the soul of black people could voice protest amid the dehumanizing and repressive constraints of white oppression, dehumanization, and racism.

Walking a different talk thus means having the power, capacity, and audacity to create for oneself legitimate forms of expression of beingness that facilitate the realization of personal potential through the actualization of human freedom and autonomy. Because African American spirituality encourages a freedom of being through the generation of free personal expression, black people have been able to establish unique idioms and configurations of a black ontology, thus precipitating their actualization as free persons in this society.

Centering Life in Divine Love

Love is a centering power of African American life. This begins with the love of God, God's love of us that extends to love of self and others. To love oneself when virtually everything in society has taught one to hate oneself is a quintessential attainment of African American freedom. African American spirituality has taught black people to love themselves unconditionally and to look to divine love as an authentic source for naming and defining their true identity and reality. African American spirituality as a totalizing, unifying soul force has helped black people overcome these various disaffections through the power of love.

Despite the negativity propagated by the media about the problems, troubles, and disparities of African Americans, the truth is there is a unifying, unquenchable love and kinship among those who are comfortable being black. Preponderant media images portray black people as a generally unruly, unhappy, malingering lot who are always at each other's throats and suggest that no good thing can ever come out of the black community. Unfortunately, there are many blacks harboring attitudes based on such negative experiences with their own people. This is true of any community. However, these untoward sentiments have not become the defining issues of black potential and personhood.

For example, the existence of crime in African American communities does not mean that all black people are criminals. Crime is simply a reality describing a condition in the black community, not a definition of the character and capacity of African American people. Other communities have crime, but the people in them are not defined in terms of the crime but by their ability to face and resolve the problem of crime. They are defined by their potential, not by their defeats. The overriding concern is the people's capacity to find a long-term solution to the maladies plaguing them, not the difficulties that temporarily flourish in their midst.

This is the history of African Americans: facing and overcoming enormous problems and odds in every aspect of their American journey. The capacity to confront and surmount these problems is due largely to their problem-solving spirituality and the ways of love taught them by their forebears. Blacks could not have come this far without having some measure of self-love. This important fact of black life has often been overshadowed by the problems and plight of black communities.

This love is expressed through joy, laughter, tears, and a sense of kinship that runs heart to heart. African American spirituality teaches blacks to love themselves and others. This has been the saving grace of black communities in America. Their struggles have united them in love. Their victories over those struggles have moved them closer to God and to each other. Without romanticizing and oversimplifying here, love has been the centering spirit and force of African American people since their beginnings in time. It has been an antidote to the cruelties and atrocities committed against them by racist whites and other adversaries who have sought to destroy them.

Key terms here are *spirit*, which is a dynamic, amorphous, life-giving, and sustaining force, and *love*, which is the assurance that one is needed, nurtured, and valued by others. Love provides a sense of importance to individuals as they live and relate within the larger human community. It establishes a place of belonging for them within that context.

An objective of African American spirituality has been to instill in black people self-love, self-respect, a sense of justice, and equality rooted in divine love. Centering black people in all-enveloping love of God has been a principal task of black spirituality. Lerone Bennett defines it this way:

> It is singing and sharing; dancing and fighting; shouting and serving; making love and making up; believing and building; rocking in ecstasy and resisting evil; teaching and politicizing; preaching and socializing; saving souls and strengthening schools; building and developing; uniting and unifying; being and becoming; it is the force within all black people that says you will not destroy my humanity, regardless of what you do.[4]

Amid conditions of hostility, persecution, discrimination, repression, rejection, seduction, denigration, devaluation, brutality, disaffection, castration, and mutilation, black people have learned to center themselves spiritually, love themselves unconditionally, maintain their dignity categorically, and defeat all attempts to dislocate, deculturate, and destroy them permanently.

This power is ensured by a spirit of love emanating from God and the universe, a love that embraces, bolsters, buoys, and ultimately supports the power of the black soul to withstand all attempts to sequester and destroy it. The spirit of love thereby becomes the ultimate unifying and centering force of black existence, giving blacks a sense of pride, power, value, and purpose in a society that has largely hated, denigrated, and devalued them as human beings. To live by love in a society that promulgates hate is an act of human freedom.

The simple practice of love among black people comes from knowing unconditionally that God loves them, notwithstanding their troubles and sorrows, and by praying constantly that God will deliver them all from fear. It also means that no other people can ultimately wield the power or authority to determine black self-worth. Because whites have lost all moral authority due to the hypocrisies of racism, as James Baldwin and others observe, they can never ethically determine for black people who they ultimately shall become.[5]

Furthermore, as children of the universe, blacks have learned to center themselves cosmically and ontologically through the power of divine love. When whites had essentially dislocated blacks by forcibly relocating them to America and thus making them aliens and strangers in their American "homeland," the power of love relocated and recentered them as citizens of the universe.

The transcendent power of divine love lifted them from the doldrums of suicidal despair and brought them relief from the perils of systemic estrangement. Such love is a force moving from soul to soul and heart to heart. It calms the mind and soothes the pain of living black in America. There is a balm in Gilead!

Love remains the centering force of African American life and a chief cornerstone of African American spirituality. To love and be loved is an expression of freedom in a society that promulgates and promotes human hatred as a way of life and self-actualization. That African Americans can still love God, themselves, and even their adversaries after being subjected to so much hatred is a supreme manifestation of black freedom in America. The antithesis of soul-consuming rage and an affirmative response to dehumanization, this love is actualized through the practice of spirituality and is one ultimate expression of self-determination.

James Baldwin in delineating the courage and love of the student movement in sixties describes it as *spiritual resilience*.[6] Sheer soul force of divine love has been a guiding impetus for black humanity, dignity, power, and self-respect. Spirituality is the catalyst igniting such sensibilities in the fray of perennial and unmitigated conflict. Sociologist Creigs Beverly, in an article on black spirituality and mental health, says:

Black spirituality gives you the strength to have hope in the midst of despair; to be confident in the face of doubt; to stand firm in the whirlwind of controversy; to see possibilities when all options appear to be exhausted; and to believe in the absence of any empirical evidence to support your beliefs.[7]

It is important to remember that because race is primordially ontological, racism assaults the basic personhood and character of a people on reasons for which they cannot be totally responsible. A person born black into the world has no choice in being black and to persecute that person because of his or her blackness is to denigrate her or him for no self-engendered reason. Racism is a form of human denigration demonstrated against people for ontological reasons.

This is very different than discriminating against persons because they are rude, obnoxious, or abrasive. Such behavior can presumably be controlled by the individual, or ascribed to personal volition. It places some responsibility on the person for evoking such animus. In other words, the individual can choose or not to be a cur. However, discriminating on the basis of skin color is a fundamental attack on the person's basic ontology, his or her basic right to be and exist as a human being in his or her own black skin. Here the human person does not have a choice of skin color. It is not of her or his own choosing and thus makes her or him the unwarranted victim of persecution.

Because white racism is such a fundamental attack on black personhood, black spirituality has had to provide a counteracting system of values and beliefs that inherently refutes all attempts to define, degrade, and ultimately destroy black self-esteem and power on the basis of race. Black spirituality has given black people the capacity to love, affirm, value, and develop themselves amid continual hostilities. By providing systems of religious belief, personal value, and morality, African American spirituality enabled black people to overcome racial constraints.

In other words, within the matrix of African American spirituality is the belief that black people are created equal to whites, that their specially created black skin so fundamental to their being and so despised by whites is the foundation of their ontological and spiritual well-being. This means if whites attack and persecute them because they are black, God loves and nurtures them in part for the very same reason.

The venom of racial hatred is thus neutralized by an omnipresent and omniscient divine love that relocates black people within the Spirit of a transcendent divine power, thus causing them to avoid personifying the same poisonous loathing of other races that has been relegated to them. That black people have experienced such abomination without fomenting the same animus toward whites can be imputed to the power of divine love mediated through the practice of black spirituality. Because blacks were identified as children of God meant that they not only had heightened expectations of what God would do for and through them but elevated anticipations of their own power and self-worth to overcome the iniquities of their environment.

The reality of divine love through the practice of black spirituality has conferred on black Americans a transcendent power of revitalization and redemption. It has instilled within them the capacity to think and act as free persons loved by God though hated by their adversaries. This is the extant truth of the ontological form of black freedom. It is freedom to be what God created one to be in a society that has attempted to restrict and define the terms of that freedom. The centering power of divine love in black life has thus precipitated the actualization of such freedom through the practice of black spirituality. The objective of dehumanization and racism is to make the oppressed like the oppressor. By choosing divine love as a means of centering black life, African Americans have repudiated their adversaries' attempts to psychologically and spiritually enslave them.

Seeing with Soul
and Feeling with Passion

Another important ontological manifestation of African American spirituality as an expression of human freedom is seeing, articulating, and expressing the feeling of black life in the Spirit. An important aspect of African American experience is seeing the passion of human existence or seeing with the soul. The soul has windows from which black people view the world around them.

Passion is a fruit of soul and an expression of soul force. To see with feeling, to embrace the deeper angularities of human sentiment, is a quality that has enabled black people to break free from the dispassion of Anglo-American cultural restraints. In other words, being in touch with one's feelings is not only a vital sign of black humanity but is also a form of personal autonomy that negates and obviates the dispassion created by the inhumanities and cruelties of white culture and racism. To feel and see is to resist the spiritual and emotional ossification and annihilation that results from white racism.

Creative and Resistant
Soul Force

In *Black and White Styles in Conflict*, Thomas Kochman observes:

Black culture allows its members considerably greater freedom to assert and express themselves than does white culture. Black cul-

ture values individually regulated self-assertion. White culture
values the ability of individuals to rein in their impulses. White
cultural events do not allow for individually initiated self-assertion
or the spontaneous expression of feeling.[8]

Freely expressing feelings is an emblem of the black culture soul and a
part of the soul force of black life. Slavery and white oppression created
and reinforced a cruel culture of silence for African Americans. The result
has been the formation of an ethos wherein the power to express oneself
fully and openly has become a hallmark of African American strength and
freedom. Black spirituality has always given African Americans the license
and power to express themselves through the sentiments and dynamism
of sheer creative and resistant soul force. Creative soul force allows black
people to create their own culture and freedom under conditions of oppression and domination. Resistant soul force refuses complete domination and domestication by those powers that be.

Because of the culture of silence and brutality of their social circumstances, blacks cultivated a propensity to see and express their feelings as
cultural subversion in a society that sought to anesthetize them to all feeling through various forms of persecution. The fact that blacks feel deeply
inside and generally have the urge to express themselves more emotionally and passionately than some white people means that blacks have re-
fused to relinquish that aspect of their being that makes them fully human
and truly free persons. The individual who has lost the ability to feel and
express life passionately is therefore not free, nor rooted in the power of
blackness that pure soul force engenders.

Through the cultivation of creative and resistant soul force, African
Americans have always sought to free themselves from those emotional
and psychological constraints that induced their emotional psychological
enslavement. The fact that they could and did express what they felt in a
society that inflicted so much pain upon them for doing so is the ultimate
act of self-determination and defiance. While whites inflicted pain on
blacks to coerce their fear, silence, and apathy, black people surmounted
these constraints by creating even greater ways of creatively expressing
their feelings and ideas through their culture and spirituality.

The ability to see with feeling in the midst of chaos, hardship, and persecution is the capacity to transcend the devastations of the environment
and the ultimate expression of humanity. To feel what one feels and to express that feeling through idioms and ethos that cannot be essentially
sanctioned, determined, or controlled by oppressors signifies the freedom
to be, to express one's inner soul against all the proscriptions and reduc-
tions of the environment.

Seeing with soul suggests a reversal or inversion of the senses. Usually we speak of feeling the feeling but seeing the feeling signifies the capacity of African Americans to invert those aspects of reality that preclude their empowerment. It symbolizes the power to exceed an analysis of the obvious and purports an ability to adopt and adapt reality according to the African soul view of the universe.

For black people the soul or soul force is the élan vital undergirding black existence. The soul is the cosmic, spiritual, ontological, epistemological center of African American existence. The soul has mind, a capacity all its own that involves the process of cogitation and intuition, analysis and sentiment, with head and heart. It is form and dynamic, spirit and matter coalescing into an élan vital, which governs, sustains, transforms, and empowers black life in its myriad forms. Soul constitutes the organizing principle of life where opposites coalesce into a unified framework of consciousness and being. Soul is the oasis of all black power and creativity. It shapes consciousness and gives wings to the human spirit. Soul articulates itself in thought and passion. It unifies thought and feeling into a life-sustaining force.

To see and express the feeling emanates from the black soul center of life. It is the capacity to feel and be felt, to think and be thought, to act and be acted upon by the ethos and larger cosmos. This soul force is a fundamental point of differentiation between blacks and whites. Blacks live, think, and have their being from this soul center. Soul force provides the ability to think, express, act, and overcome. The expression of feeling fully and truthfully is the ultimate expression of personal freedom to the person who has been physically and emotionally repressed. To see and express the feeling passionately signifies the freedom to be in response to the repressions of racism and oppression. Such soul force is manifested in every aspect of black culture and spirituality and is a definitive factor shaping the African American paradigm of freedom.

Seeing the feeling is not simply an oppositional response to white racism in America but a mode of orientation of black people to reality in general. Not every cultural and spiritual modality in black life is a response to white racism. Black life has its own ethos, norms, values, and behaviors that shape black existence independent of the constraints of white racism and oppression. Soul is an emblem of black life in America. This soul force ranges from the soulful preaching of black ministers to the soulful way that black people walk, talk, dress, think, and act. There is a poetry of the soul that black life in America exudes. It is found in black laughter, in tearful and joyous hugs or high fives; it permeates the music, culture, and spirituality of African Americans. This soul is intimately tied to the soul of the universe. The universe has its soulful rhythms from the cadences of the sea to the melodies of birds. Soul is emblematic of the harmony of the universe, and black people express that soul as a way of establishing that harmony and staying in touch with God.

Seeing with feeling is not only a value in black life but a norm of human and ontological interaction. Black relationships pattern themselves on those configurations of sentiment and belief that issue from a much broader spectrum of reality than can be conceived prima facie. In other words, the cognitive patterns constituting the foundation of black interaction are not modalities emerging from the mind only but also from that vast corpus of human being that envelops and exceeds normative cognitive configurations. The fact that one can see the feeling and act upon it suggests that the empirical sources of behavior are much greater than the conventional cognitive sources conceived in the Western worldview.

It means that African Americans' entire ontological orientation toward reality draws from a vast constellation of resources both spiritual and material, which allow them not only to embrace but exceed the ontological constraints imposed on them by others. Seeing the feeling is grasping the broader basis of human being and interaction subliminal to customary ways of knowing and being. Soul is the means by which they interpret, grasp, and sense reality.

To see the passion or feeling is to operate from a different ontological mode of existence as an oppositional response to the normative cognitive and behavioral patterns of white culture and society. For black people the seeing must not only be felt but demonstrated in ways in which it can be seen by others as a means of communicating thoughts, ideas, attitudes, and feelings.

To put this still another way, we might say that passion and feeling are invaluable modes for the communication of ideas in black life and culture. Ideas not only shape and evoke their own realities, but sentiments also create and express their own thoughts and meanings. Feelings embrace and propel ideas as vital expressions of human being. Passion therefore is not only a significant source in the transmission of ideas and concepts but is also a means of seeing, grasping, and imprinting the self on the larger reality of selves. This is made possible by creative soul force.

This mode of black ontology has been essential to African American freedom, not only because it preserves an autonomy of the soul to be and express itself in opposition to the repressive dehumanization and culture of silence of white racism, but also because it preserves a unique way for blacks to orient and imprint themselves on the larger cosmos so as to transcend the ontological and epistemological constraints locally imposed by various processes of oppression.

Seeing with passion is not only a manifestation of the black soul force spirit but a vehicle by which the black soul can be used by the Spirit to more adequately express its ideas, power, and purpose in reality. In European thought, ideas may convey passion, but in African thought, passion more adequately expresses the force of ideas. The Spirit speaks through convincing thought, the embodiment of ideas in human sentiment that creates its own unique ethos. Dona Richards explains it this way:

> The idea of *spirit* is especially important for an appreciation of the African-American experience. Spirit is, of course, not a rationalistic concept. It cannot be quantified, measured, explained by or reduced to neat, rational, conceptual categories as Western thought demands. Spirit is ethereal. It is neither touched nor moved, seen nor felt in the way that physical entities are touched, moved, seen and felt. . . . Our spirit symbolizes our uniqueness as a people, or we could say that the African-American ethos is spiritual.[9]

This mode of ontological orientation where blacks can see the feeling establishes its own ethos, culture, and cognitive framework for black existence. The field force of human sentiment is a much more fertile resource for the cultivation and dissemination of ideas. The passion or feeling of black life is an important fount of black culture, creativity, and spirituality not only because it is a rich source of ideas but also because it provides a much wider spectrum for the communication of the multiplicity of dynamics, trajectories, and forms of the African American ethos.

Seeing the feeling is thereby a form of creativity. It is a mode of improvisation and innovation as a foundation of black life and freedom. To see the feeling and express it through soul and various creative idioms of thought and sentiment is to create a world in which the being as stranger and outsider finds its place amid the forces of estrangement and alienation. The feelings that are thus seen are translated into idioms and configurations of value and meaning that help black people recenter and relocate themselves spiritually in a society that has rejected them ontologically.

Since the soul is the key to ontological well-being in black life and culture, and it preserves black creativity as a vital force, the retention of soul autonomy and creativity is essential to maintaining black identity, sanity, and survival. That black people choose to orient to reality on these terms is a further manifestation of black freedom.

This aspect of black ontology and freedom is very significant. Seeing helps to establish one's place in the world and seeing with feeling is the way African Americans establish themselves in the American context. It is a unique autonomy that provides blacks with a peculiar way of orienting, grasping, and making sense of their environment. To live with passion and feeling for life is a hallmark of African American experience, for the passion to be is synonymous with the passion to fulfill what one is and desires to be in a world that negates that being through dispassion and dehumanization.

Seeing with soul and feeling with passion affirms black people's desire to affirm their humanness under conditions of dehumanization. It rejuvenates the spirit of African Americans and establishes their powerful place within the human family.

Praxis Faith

At the core of African American spirituality that has facilitated the development of a unique black ontology is the practice of unwavering faith in God. That black people still exist in America is an expression of unyielding faith in a power greater than life. Ontology is directly related to faith. For African Americans faith and being thus go hand in hand.

In a society that has singled them out and persecuted them for obvious biological, racial, and ontological reasons, black Americans have cultivated the practice of faith as an emblem of personhood and a means of survival. It is very difficult to imagine a people undergoing such thoroughgoing racism and discrimination for so long without having something to help them get over the trials and perils of their human condition.

Black being and practicing faith have to do with garnering the power to get up in the morning and face each new day with the conviction that God will see them through despite the storms of human experience. Having faith simply means possessing the power to hold on and hold out, to trust God in all things and claim unequivocal belief that despite the slings and arrows of outrageous misfortune, God is still in charge and everything will work out in the by and by. Practicing faith is relying on a transcendent power to guide one through the difficulties of life. African Americans have had to rely upon it to survive from day to day. To be black in America means to practice some form of spiritual faith and belief, to claim such belief as indispensable to black sanity, well-being, and survival. We cannot imagine black life in America without this significant aspect of black spirituality. It is because of the prayers and faith of those who have gone before us and are with us that we are able to enjoy some semblance of human freedom today.

Thus faith is not simply an idea or a potion pulled off the shelf for use in hard times. It is a living part of the litany of black life in America. It is living with the belief that the oppressed will triumph over oppressors and justice shall be requited to those treated unjustly. The practice of faith equally means that spiritual belief is at the core of black consciousness, culture, and spirituality in America. This theme of having, keeping, and practicing faith is perhaps the most prominent in African American life. Every political, social, or spiritual movement of African Americans has some faith as its beacon light. The civil rights, black nationalist, and other movements all have stressed the value of faith in the lives of African Americans.

In terms of consciousness, faith is the bedrock of black knowledge, understanding, and belief. Faith takes the unknown and unseen and translates it into realizable possibilities. It creates hope and desire to live as fully human and engenders a propensity to strive constantly to realize one's greatest potential. Practicing faith as a foundation of consciousness means that black people have had to believe in God and in their own power to transform their existential condition. The black mind is conditioned by faith, and black spirituality has instilled in black people the necessity of living faithfully through all things.

Culturally, faith is the catalyst for new and creative ideas. It is a galvanizing force for the free expression of black spirituality and belief. Faith means telling it like it is and living hopefully in the present. It means not accepting "no" for an answer from the larger society but affirming a "yes, I can" in response. Creating alternative prisms of expression and being is also an insignia of faith.

From the beginning of black existence in America the reality of faith has shaped, empowered, and sustained the lives of African Americans. It is the single most important spiritual resource of black people in America. Without faith, blacks would have relinquished to the forces of racism and oppression years ago either by destroying themselves more actively by suicide and genocide or by wallowing in the doldrums of complete, unmitigated lethargy and despair.

To be black in America therefore is to believe in God. To live faithfully and spiritually in black America is to demonstrate the reality and presence of God. Given the tumultuous history of African Americans in this country, we could not have come this far without practicing faith as an integral part of our basic ontology.

The principal characteristics of black ontology as it relates to black spirituality as a practice of freedom are (1) living the truth of black existence, (2) walking a different talk, (3) centering life in divine love, (4) seeing with soul and feeling with passion, and (5) practicing faith. While there are numerous other ontological modalities related to acting, thinking, and being in general, these most adequately reflect black being and the practice of spirituality as a paradigm of human freedom. The practice of spirituality provides the perseverance and preservation of black life as soul force in American society.

Four

Spirituality and
Freeing Relationships

A significant aspect of African American spirituality as a practice of human freedom is the establishment of cooperative and harmonious relationships as the basis of black community. At the heart of black freedom is the idea of the human person as a vital link in community with other persons. A. Okechukwu Ogbonnaya, in his article, "Person as Community: An African Understanding of the Person as Intrapsychic Community," observes that "the community and its centers of vitality are the beginning and end of the individual. The person, too, is an integrating entity. The person has a principle of vitality as does the community. This center of vitality for the individual harmonizes and connects the community within the individual in the African worldview."[1]

Ogbonnaya refers to Kwesi Dickson to underscore the importance of community in the African worldview: "A society (community) is in equilibrium when its customs are maintained, its goals attained and spirit powers given regular and adequate recognition. Members of society (community) are expected to live and act in such a way as to promote society's well-being; to do otherwise is to court disaster, not only for the individual actor but for community as a whole."[2]

The individual is a community unto himself or herself but also participates in a larger community of other selves. For black people, being part of a larger social aggregate gives collective strength and vitality. Positive relationships are manifested in black relationships in general, in the black family and extended family, and in the development of an ethos where all blacks are actually and potentially viewed as persons of inestimable worth. Evan M. Zuesse observes: "Reality is not being, contrary to the prevalent Christian idea, but in relationship. The more one ties things together, the more power and transcendence, for power flows through relationships. The goal of life, then, is to maintain and join the cosmic web that holds and sustains all things and beings, to be part of the integral mutuality of things."[3]

Harmony and equilibrium are realized in the formation of positive relationships among black people through the practice of spirituality that affirms their ultimate sanctity and worth as persons. The corporate experience of black spiritual practice has historically provided a context in which the value of persons could be affirmed in the larger community. Not only does the context of black spirituality empower blacks to coexist harmoniously among themselves and others, but its corporate practice in the life of the church and community provides opportunities for the establishment and strengthening of African American community. Black people convening to praise God and celebrate life create a basis for reinforcing group identity and communal solidarity. Spiritual praxis makes this possible.

Essential to the establishment of a vital community among black people is the development of a culture or ethos of positive relationships that facilitate the realization of human potential and establish a black cooperative network of collective soul force.

Life as Invocation and Affirmation

The Spirit of God is the ultimate spiritual life force permeating and unifying African American communities into a harmonious whole. Divine Spirit and soul force make the establishment of black community possible. African American spiritual praxis requires that individuals within the community invoke and call down the Spirit of God as a foundation for establishing community. Life in the Spirit is indispensable to the formation of consciousness, culture, identity, and community, which lays the foundation for the consolidation and transformation of community. While blacks view themselves as an integral part of a larger diverse whole, the formation of community through strong communal and familial relationships is the cornerstone of African American existence.

Black life then is a perpetual invocation of the Spirit power, presence, and work to overcome communal distinction and harmonize its disparate parts into a community of wholeness, strength, and potential. Without the Spirit of God, black people could not overcome the constraints of disintegration, oppression, and dehumanization. Divine Spirit is the basis of the black community and a source of its collective power and strength. Communing in the Spirit overcomes the disparities of the African American community and allows black people to forge a common ground with themselves and others.

Practicing the Spirit and creative presence of God is still the most powerful ritual of African American life. Using that Spirit to build community is the paramount focus of African American spirituality. Black people call upon the Spirit daily as a source of hope and sustenance and affirm its power as essential to the survival of African American communities.

Thus the Spirit's working and God's creative presence is the foundation to black consciousness, belief, and behavior and the fundamental catalyst for establishing and solidifying relationships among blacks. The Spirit instills within African Americans an appreciation of God who undergirds and empowers communal life.

A fundamental strength of African American life is not only to know and affirm God's Spirit but to practice God's creative presence as a basis for consolidating, developing, and harmonizing African American people. To envelop oneself in the power of God's Spirit and to disseminate that Spirit as a means of creating and sustaining community is very important for the health, wholeness, and vitality of blacks in America.

Rappin', Signifyin', and Testifyin'

Another important emblem of black freedom in America is the power of black people to rap, signify, and testify. Oral culture is predominant in African American communities where the spoken word is a powerful medium for ordering the chaos and problems of human existence. Having the power to rap, signify, and testify is an important element of freedom in a culture that values the profundity of oral communication. These three modes of dialogue symbolize the capacity to think intelligently, act decisively, and express creatively and courageously the feelings black people harbor about life in America.

Rappin'

Rappin' is a powerful force for establishing and sustaining viable human relations among African Americans. The power of rap is not only in the message communicated but in the audacity of the communicator to speak his or her mind openly, freely, and sometimes profanely. Rappin' may be viewed as a means of conjuring or litanizing the realities of black existence into harmonious forms and idioms that help make sense of the absurdities of black life in America. Geneva Smitherman tells us that black rap has been used to challenge, overcome, and even devastate enemies.[4] Perhaps the genesis of rap was on the plantations when slaves spun tales, told stories, and conjured lines that would simulate their quest for human freedom. The slave preacher was a rapper par excellence, and slaves would rap among themselves as a means of lamenting and escaping the blight of slavery.

The power of rap lies in its ability to affirm and reject, maintain and transform the status quo. The black church has preserved the dynamics of religious and spiritual rap throughout African American history. The sanity, solace, liberation, and transformation of black people directly stems from the power of deacons, preachers, mothers, grandmothers, grandfathers, and fathers to rap to the Lord each day of the week in the form of prayers, songs, testifying, and various other litanies. Spiritual rap was perfected under the auspices of African American spiritual praxis.

Equally important is the power of rap as a liberating and healing force for black people because words have their own power, create their own realities, dispense their own cures, and verbally rectify atrocities and injustice. What cannot be conquered socially can be overcome verbally through the power of rap. Black people believe and affirm the power of the spoken word, and this has been an important aspect of black relational and communal empowerment. As a force for vital liberation in African American communities, spiritual rappin' has brought many a soul from darkness and freed many a prisoner from bondage.

Not only is the power of spiritual rappin' actualized in the rhythm, cadence, and majesty of words but in their ability to influence and modify behavior. Words have power. Words spoken poetically in the rhythms and verse of black culture have an even more powerful affect on hearers.

Rappin' is an antithesis to white culture and expression. White people as a rule do not or choose not to rap. Black rap is a form of spiritual and verbal alchemy that transforms reality and empowers the rapper. In an oral culture where words possess power, authority, and "magic," rappin' has an important function. It not only enables the speaker to name, describe, and define reality but also to control purposes and outcomes through the use of words.

Black spirituality has always valued the power of the spoken word in shaping black consciousness, building black communities, and enabling black people to transform their spiritual and existential condition. Black culture and black spirituality could not have emerged without rap, and many black people have been saved, redeemed, and transformed by it. Rappin' freely and creatively preserves the ability of the person to call it like she or he sees it, and this is an important element in preserving personal freedom.

Moreover, every significant cultural, spiritual, and political movement by blacks in America has been led by a gifted orator or one who knows how to rap to black audiences. Frederick Douglass, Henry Highland Garnet, Paul Robeson, Ida B. Wells, Marcus Garvey, Malcolm X, Martin Luther King Jr., H. Rap Brown, Stokely Carmichael, James Forman, and even Louis Farrakhan today are magnificent rappers. Their words can move black audiences in ways that positively transform black Americans.

Rappin' is not only a form of communication but a predominant mode of black linguistic freedom. Virtually every plantation had a storyteller or rapper, a person who could speak words so powerfully and eloquently that even slave masters could be periodically moved to tears or joy. This person would also occasionally speak for slaves who found themselves in a particular quandary. They could intercede on behalf of black slaves who incurred their master's disfavor. The gift of oral communication has thus been a saving, liberating, and redemptive force of African Americans throughout their history. When masters brutalized them, black slaves ventilated by rappin' about their feelings. When the oppression and trials of black life on plantations became unbearable, the slave preacher rapped about how God would fix things, and black audiences in worship rapped about their plight through prayers, shouting, and other forms of verbal communication. Rappin' had a therapeutic or medicinal function on plantations as in black life today. The power of rap issues from the soul. The capacity of the communicator to express with spiritual and rhythmic power the deeper longings of the mind, heart, and spirit brought release and power to black souls who found themselves sequestered and blistered by dehumanizing circumstances. Spiritual rap thus had a significant place in African American spiritual praxis.

Furthermore, possessing the audacity to rap in a culture of repression and silence was an expression of black freedom. The content of rap was often coded with meanings, symbols, and figurations that expressed the terms and conditions of black freedom. Evidence of this is manifested both in the content and forms of the music, lyrics, prayers, sermons, and other media in African American life and culture. Black spiritual power resides not only in what is said but in how it is said that moves black audiences to positive and constructive action.

Spiritual rap has thus always been an integral part of African American spiritual practice because it allows the communicator to express his or her persona and being through creative soul force. It equally encourages individuals to shape the chaos and uncertainties of reality through verbalization and enables them to name, define, and transform reality through the power of words. Words can change perceptions and reality and can transform internal and external conditions.

The power of rap is that it has been a liberating and humanizing force in the practice of African American spirituality. As stated earlier, rap was a liberating force for African Americans on the plantation. While racism had virtually decided their fate and limited their access to the amenities of society, rap became a creative tool of the mind and spirit urging black people to transcend their social condition. It exhorted black people to escape reality through the conjuring of words. The efficacy of such words cannot be overestimated, for healing, solace, and sanity were created for blacks in the midst of volatile circumstances.

Rap has had both a humanizing and militating influence on African Americans. The practice of spirituality and its use of rap mostly enabled blacks to construct a universe or world in which they could verbalize and respond to their conditions on their own terms. The value of rap lies in the way it has encouraged black people to make sense of their plight, to adopt, adapt, and transform reality through the creative power of words. It is safe to say that black people could not have come this way without healing, loving, and admonishing, life-lifting words. Black rappin' is thus a form of spiritual alchemy actualized as a creative soul force for freedom.

The black rapper—whether preacher, musician, teacher, or politician—has always been a critical exponent of freedom for black Americans. African American spirituality is the cultural and spiritual seedbed of African American oratorical gifts, and rap has always had a central place in its formation and development.

Equally significant is the power of rap in shaping relational outcomes and empowering community action. We stated earlier that rap is a relational and communal form of human freedom for African Americans. The gift of gab or oratory is a central élan in black life. The heartbeat of every African American community pulsates on the drum or bass beat of conversation, dialogue, or rap. African American oratory and verbalization is the lifeblood of black communities. Visit any black neighborhood and you will find the power of words reverberating and permeating the culture, air, movement, and ethos of African American people.

Everywhere there are words, and words teem with power. There is life and vitality in words. Words not only have their own power but create their own rhythms and litanies of life that creates sacred discourse among black people. Within African American dialogical structures is a call and response for harmony, unity, and love among black people. Words create community, conditions, and terms of endearment. They establish the ethos in which reciprocity and intimacy are allowed to emerge. The power of black rap lies also in its capacity to create community through relationships in which words possess their own magic and archives of truth informing and shaping black reality.

We cannot imagine black culture and black spirituality without seriously considering the power of words in shaping reality. We further cannot conceive of the formation and perpetuation of black relationships and communities without the presence of dynamic, empowering words, words that heal, liberate, and transform both the individual and community.

The significance of rap as a force for black freedom is the way it has exhorted and enabled black people to transform adversity and pain into tranquility and gain. The words of black rappers have reached so deep inside the minds and souls of black hearers so as to help them translate their experience into a wholesome and meaningful reality. Words that get on the inside of black hearts, minds, and souls have again enabled black people to spiritually transcend the perils of dehumanization. Rap has helped black people make sense of their reality, create systems of meaning and power that facilitate their long-term sanity, liberation, and survival.

Signifyin'

If spiritual rap has been a vital force for the freedom of black Americans both individually and communally, the power of signifyin' is equally so. In his monumental work *The Signifying Monkey*, Henry Louis Gates, Jr., uses a definition of signifying developed by Roger D. Abrahams: "The same 'Signifying Monkey' shows (the hero) to be a trickster, 'signifying' being the language of trickery, that set of words or gestures which arrives at 'direction through indirection'."[5]

"Arriving at direction through indirection" is not only a means for keeping the advantage over adversaries but also exemplifies an ingenuity and intelligence that ably manipulates the hegemonic or dominant powers. One who signifies has not only used great creativity and imagination to arrive at direction but has a certain contempt for those whom he is signifyin'.

The power of signifyin' in African American communities lies not only in the esoteric aspects of language and codification used to communicate ideas but in the ferocity, humor, and vitriol in which the message is communicated. It is our contention that signifyin' has been an important dimension of the relational and communal forms of African American freedom because of the way it has allowed black people to arrive at the direction of freedom through indirection. We might say without oversimplifying that African American spirituality as the practice of freedom has always contained a certain signifying element in relation to the dominant culture and society.

Black slaves signified on white masters and on each other. Emerging here then is a kind of culture of ingenuity, deception, and contempt that affirms the right of the black individual to call it like he or she sees it, notwithstanding the larger culture's power to name and define the reality of black life. The practice of African American spirituality retained a form of signification in its creation of black culture. We see it manifested in black music, sermonizing, and storytelling as viable expressions of freedom.

To *signify* is thus to discard or embrace the conventions of Anglo culture through processes of verbalization. It is to practice and arrive at a reality of freedom, dignity, and meaning through conjuring, imagining, and dissembling. To signify is to express the core of personal freedom that both embraces and refutes existing reality.

Black preaching, music, culture, and creativity have all epitomized various signification processes. The practice of black spirituality as a soul force for human freedom emerges from a basic culture of contempt that black people have had for their human condition. If slavery and oppression could not be immediately transformed, it could thereby be changed through the power of words that blasted and belittled every attempt at black subjugation. If freedom could not be attained externally in reality, it could be won internally in the hearts, minds, spirits of black individuals and black communities on the landscape of the soul, in the infrastructures of the human spirit, in the courtesies of culture, wherein the power of words could liberate, transform, and ultimately repudiate all forms of dehumanization, domination, and spiritual domestication.

To signify is ultimately to defy that which negates and questions black people's right to be and live as whole and human persons in a racist soci-ety. Again words create the context for the liberation of the mind, soul, and heart of black people in order to create a reality of dignity and power through the field force of verbalization. What cannot be achieved in real-ity is made up for in words. What cannot be achieved socially, politically, or economically is attained culturally, spiritually, and verbally. Freedom of creative and resistant soul force is still experienced because of the power of words to liberate.

While the body is enslaved, the mind, spirit, imagination, and soul are free to create and conjure, to construct a viable reality wherein the person is really set free from the constraints, conventions, and centers of power that seemingly control his or her fate and destiny. Words, therefore, are not a substitute for material and physical freedom but simply open the darkened corridors of the mind, heart, and soul where black people have found freedom, solace, and sanity amid the fury and fires of a racist soci-ety. The signifier through words undermines the capacity of oppressors to linguistically name, define, and control reality through processes of ver-balization, conceptualization, and social construction. Oppressors then will never have the last word because the signifier will ultimately turn up-side down all that dominators claim to be right side up. Signifyin' is the antithesis of the language of power and domination wherein processes of subjugation are linguistically disseminated through the structures, id-ioms, symbols, and meanings of the powerful. The language of oppres-sors reinforces the system of oppression. The language of black significa-tion subverts that system through linguistic inversion and conquest and the general defiance of the larger culture and society.

African American spirituality has always enabled black people to cul-tivate a language of spirituality that establishes and reinforces their own freedom, power, and models of human transformation. The role of the signifier is not only to signify in response to various forms of domination but to orally create systems of value and meaning that will perpetuate the idioms of black creativity and freedom. To signify is not only to defy the larger culture through the antithetical and oppositional use of culture and language but to create orally idioms and nuances of meaning that escape the machinations, hegemony, and manipulation of those in power.

African American spirituality as a force for black freedom has always been highly verbal, underscoring not only the power of words to shape re-ality and defy domination but to create an ethos of language, methods, and configurations that through their oppositional practice establish and reinforce black spiritual and cultural freedom. The ultimate freedom is for the soul to fully and creatively express itself in defiance to those systems of cultural domination and oppression. In other words, black people can never fully be subjugated by their oppressors so long as they possess the power to create their own reality through the use of language, forms, and modalities that negate their own oppression. Signifyin' is an excellent example of such freedom.

Not only is the content oppositional to conventional language modalities by arriving at direction through indirection, but so are the forms that through repetition create their own archives of truth and authority that legitimate them as a praxis of black freedom. The content and forms of signifyin' thus have important implications for African American freedom. *What* is said is significant. *How* it is said is vital. *That* it is said as a practice of black culture and spirituality is essential to the establishment and routinization of black freedom in America.

Some of the more outstanding examples of signifyin' through more formal discourse are Frederick Douglass's "The Meaning of the 4th of July for the Negro," delivered in 1852 at the Rochester Ladies Anti-Slavery Society, or Malcolm X's *Ballots or Bullets,* or Henry Highland Garnet's "Let Your Motto Be Resistance." While these speeches are more formal depictions of black signification in its highest forms, they represent the capacity of the black orator to defy conventional wisdom and boldly transcend the parameters of the status quo while exhorting hearers to positive change.

We might further assert that each form of signifyin', whether formal or informal, that culminates in subtle, verbal diatribe against some custom or code of the establishment is an expression of black freedom. Perhaps the greatest signifier in the religious sense is the black preacher about whom we will say more later. Many forms of black sermonizing contain various examples of signification against the ills and evils of an oppressive system. In the days of slavery sermons were often, like their musical counterparts, replete with codes and symbols signifyin' black people's quest for social and economic freedom.

The power of signifyin' as it relates to black freedom is that often black people understood the language of signification. Black folklore and culture are filled with tales of tricksters—Brer Rabbit, for example—who speak in language unintelligible to their oppressors and are adept at outsmarting them. Wit for wit and word for word, the trickster or signifier has no match or rival. Even master is fooled and foiled by the wiles of the signifier.

Signifyin' is not only a salient aspect of African American freedom but also reinforces the power of oral tradition as an important part of black life and culture. Oral preponderance is established through verbal combat or elusion while implication and inference are vital tools for overcoming psychological subjugation. So long as one can talk, hold one's ground, and stand alone by verbalizing feelings, aspirations, defiance, and contempt, he or she can never be totally psychologically vanquished by oppressors. Because oral culture is so important to black people, it is highly imperative that no adversary ever be more orally adept than blacks. Rappin' and signifyin' are the black belts of black oral communication and culture, and the quest for freedom must have at its helm somebody who can say it, tell it like it is, and say it with unmitigated, creative soul force and power.

Black culture and black spirituality have always prized the power of the spoken word and helped create an ethos where such power can be actualized daily through various processes of human interaction, culminating in those relational and communal forms of black freedom that establish human wholeness. Words heal, defy, clarify, transform, redeem, and liberate black people from the perils of oppression. Great is he or she who can speak with power and authority in the rhythms and nuances of African American life and culture.

Testifyin'

Testifyin' is a relational and communal form of black freedom because it is always done in the context of a larger community. The basic communal truth of testifyin', as with rappin' or signifyin', is that it presupposes the presence of more than one person for the communication to have meaning.

Testifyin' is important not only because it continually invokes the power and presence of God as the primary fount of human activity, but also because it creates an ethos wherein mutual sharing of ultimate concerns facilitates communal empowerment processes. One not only talks about what God has done in one's life but also witnesses to the power of that same God in the lives of other people.

Testifyin' is simply active and faithful witnessing to God's work in one's life, for bearing witness helps establish a basis and context for the emergence of community. At the heart of every African American community, then, is a common story based on a collective revelation of the people's understanding of themselves in relation to each other and divine reality. That black people have come together to testify to the goodness of God in their lives is of immense personal value and has sustained them through the many dangers, toils, and snares of the black experience in America.

Testifyin' is not only to verbalize what God has done but to establish an ethos where the common affirmation of divine reality establishes the strength and power of a community's collective identity and purpose. Testifyin' heals and brings together people of diverse persuasions and helps forge common spiritual ground.

One of the great gifts of the African American church is the way it has encouraged black people to develop and share continual testimonies about God's love and truth in their lives. Testifyin' is an important element in helping black people cultivate and interpret themselves as a collective community. It also enables the search for deeper spiritual meaning and power in relation to the troubles, sorrows, and pain of black life. The more black people have expressed their testimonies of God in the larger community, the more they have been able to collectively cope with the adversities confronting them.

African American spirituality has always stressed the importance of black people testifying and witnessing to the power and glory of God's work in their lives. Testifyin' not only builds common ground but strengthens the bonds of communal solidarity. Again Geneva Smitherman, in *Talkin' and Testifyin': The Language of Black America*, defines testifying as follows: "*Testifyin'*, concept referring to a ritualized form of black communication in which the speaker gives verbal witness to the efficacy, truth, and power of some experience in which all blacks have shared."[6] Again the sanctity and power of oral communication in black communities is affirmed. Despite the problems, sorrows, and troubles of human existence, black believers affirm that testifyin' is not only healing but liberating. To talk about what God has done, is doing, and will do despite a personal hell on earth is transforming and liberating for the mind, body, and soul.

Sigmund Freud coined the term "talking cure." The talking cure as manifested in rappin', signifyin', and testifyin' has always been an important aspect of African American spiritual practice. That black people can even witness to the power of God in their lives after all they have endured attests to the miraculous intervention of God in their lives.

The history of African Americans might be conceived as a prolonged attempt by adversaries to rob them of the power of divine testimony. Just as rappin' and signifyin' are expressions of freedom in a highly verbal or oral culture, testimony exemplifies the freedom of black people to view and shape themselves in accordance to divine entreaty and volition. Testifyin' not only perpetually grounds them in an appreciation of God's work in their lives but corroborates the sovereignty, spirit, and power of God in their lives in spite of what has happened to them.

The power of testifyin' means that however oppressive, repulsive, and troublesome life becomes, God will always have the final say in all human affairs. That black people were able to retain a testimony amid the trials and evils of this life means they were able to ward off complete decimation by their enemies. As one saint in the church remarked, "So long as I can testify about what God means to me and the good things God has done in my life, I can maintain a measure of freedom and dignity as a human being."[7]

This statement encapsulates the basic truth of testifyin' as a form of oral communication of African American communities, for testifyin' is to affirm

God as the ultimate authority and supreme sovereign in black life. Testi-fyin' then can be seen as a form of "protest" against domination by the larger culture. It affirms God as the sole source of power in black life. This means that however repressive and oppressive life becomes, oppressors will not have complete control over black people so long as they testify and have a testimony. Testifyin' places black people in touch with the reality of God and affirms God as the supreme hegemonic reality of black life.

The power of oral defiance of the larger culture and its myriad forms of oppression and subjugation cannot be overestimated. African American spirituality has always embraced the necessity of preserving and cultivat-ing black oral traditions as expressions of freedom in relation to the larger culture. So long as black people can talk the talk and say it with power, au-thority, and influence, they can never be completely overcome by their ad-versaries.

The preservation of oral culture and communication and its attending powers has been a vehicle of freedom for black people in America, for as long as they can talk about their trials and woes, express their anger and contempt against the established order, and clearly articulate their desires and blueprints of salvation and liberation, they can remain a spiritually free people. The power and gift of oral communication through rappin', signifyin', and testifyin' has been created, preserved, and cultivated through the idioms and praxis of black culture and black spirituality.

The practice of these various modes of communication in African American communities not only preserves black consciousness and iden-tity but creates an ethos of one-upmanship in relation to oppressors and adversaries. The gift of speech is basic to one's humanity, and freedom will always be realized as long as black people can rap, signify, and tes-tify. African American communities have always fathomed the depth of their power and resources in terms of their capacity for oral communica-tion. When nobody is rappin' about the problem, signifyin' on those who created the problem, or testifyin' about the God who is helping to resolve the problem, the community has trouble defining or addressing the criti-cal issues confronting it. Because words have their own magic, influence, political and social power in predominantly oral cultures, the capacity of words to transform and change existing reality cannot be negated. This is why rappin', signifyin', and testifyin' are so indispensable to black free-dom. African American spiritual praxis has preserved these rites and rit-uals by shaping a culture whereby freedom could be realized through the practice of those idioms of oral communication that reinforce black iden-tity, consciousness, wholeness, and vitality.

African American spirituality has thus created an ethos wherein the preponderance of oral culture in black communities could be sustained as a means of defying, transcending, and transforming the structures of oppression and domination in white America. By preserving the power of rappin', signifyin', and testifyin' as oral means of building and reinforcing solidarity in African American communities, African American spirituality has again functioned as a liberating and consolidating force for black freedom. The point here is that so long as an oral people can create and maintain structures of linguistic communication that defy attempts to completely subjugate, exploit, and dehumanize them, and as long as they can orally name, define, and transcend reality for themselves in opposition to such domination, they can truly be free. African American spirituality has established this as an important aspect of the African American paradigm of human freedom. By helping maintain the hegemony of oral culture and communication among black people, it has provided them with implements to thwart their complete domestication. As long as black people come together to pray, testify, rap, signify, teach, preach, and reach under the banner of African American spiritual praxis, they can maintain a measure of personal soul autonomy in relation to their dreadful reality.

Thus to rap, signify, and testify is not only to name and define reality for oneself in a culture of racism and oppression but also to defy the capacity of other human persons to completely domesticate and dominate them in all forms of human existence. This important dimension of black freedom in America has been a saving grace for African Americans, for as long as we can rap, signify, and testify, we can maintain a measure of personal autonomy and communal hegemony in opposition to the larger culture of domination, racism, and exploitation.

The Power of Call and Response

The results of rappin', signifyin', and testifyin' as expressions of human freedom point to a larger, more important dimension of black culture and black spirituality and that is the pattern of call and response endemic to African American culture and communities. Joseph L. White observes:

> These interdependent relationships and social networks are connected across time and space by oral tradition, the power of the spoken word. The spoken word, the language of African Americans, represents a solid participatory space in which speaker and listener affirm each other's presence within the context of a call and response dialogue.[8]

The power of call and response lies not only in the content of the message that incites such mutual dialogical interaction between African

Americans but also in its forms that serve as catalysts for ritualizing and routinizing communal power and solidárity. What we mean here is that call and response patterns exemplified in African American spiritual praxis are means of rallying the community around specific concerns and ritualizing the practice of social unity and cohesion through various ceremonial and religious practices. The following is an example.

SPEAKER: "And there will come a time when we will see another day."

AUDIENCE: "That's right. We will!"

SPEAKER: "And nobody will turn us 'round when that day comes!"

AUDIENCE: "That's right, say it!"

SPEAKER: "Whatever we want to say, we got to say that God is in charge of this thing and can't no person, mind, nor mule stand in God's way when God decides to do something!"

AUDIENCE (applause): "You know you right. That's right. Go 'head. Say it!"

SPEAKER: "So let's stand up and take action! Let's stand up to those drug dealers and run them out of town because this is God's place and we are God's people. If we take two steps, God will take ten on our behalf!"

AUDIENCE: "That's it! Let's do it! Let's go. God is with us!"

The speaker spoke words and the audience responded with affirmation and approval. This is an important aspect of black oral culture and communication. Not only did words quicken responses from the audience, but the process of call and response itself has ritual significance in simulating unity and solidarity among people whose basic strength is in unified belief and action. The strength and power of African American communities resides in the notion of collective unity, notwithstanding great diversity. Black people must be unified in the practice of freedom from white racism, oppression, and other forms of domination. Collective unity and strength are reinforced through call and response patterns. Black people are not only unified around a common theme but express that unity in verbal and oral responses to the messenger. Such patterns establish a unified framework for the practice of collective consciousness.

This call and response pattern is manifested in every aspect of black communication and culture from personal conversations to Sunday morning worship. To say something and have someone respond with a "yeah," "amen," or "uh-huh" is part of the oral patterns of black culture. This response creates an ethos of kinship, unity, and reciprocity among black people. It signifies that what is said is clearly understood and creates a context for establishing community around mutually shared interests and concerns.

Perhaps the practice of call and response in black oral culture and communication has done more to reinforce expectations of black unity, community, and solidarity than other social pattern in African American life. To say something and have it corroborated and legitimized in the course of conversation is to establish a nexus of unity from which bona fide community emerges. The practice of call and response is an integral part of African American spirituality and culture, and rappin', signifyin', and testifyin' epitomize the power of words to shape, define, and transform African American reality for a positive and constructive purpose.

Rappin', signifyin', and testifyin', and call and response patterns in African American communities and culture are vital expressions of human freedom. In a society where the forms of oppression are reinforced through various language modalities and structures, an important aspect of black freedom is creating, expressing, and reconfiguring a language that embraces but transcends the dominant modes of communication as vehicles for personal freedom. This is why black Americans have always been bilingual. They can speak the king's English but have also developed language patterns uniquely their own. Such patterns facilitate socialization, create a context for community empowerment, and reinforce black identity and black consciousness. To cultivate such linguistic patterns and configurations in defiance of the dominant culture is a significant aspect of African American freedom. To develop a language that negates complete domestication while simultaneously creating and preserving community integrity and empowerment is a vital dimension of black survival in America. African American spirituality has played an important role in creating the context and culture from which these various modes of communication emerge and are sustained.

Language and linguistic patterns create contexts for socialization and interaction among a people. In African American communities these various forms of communication and expression are integral to black consciousness, identity, and freedom. In fact we could not fathom African American spirituality and culture without rappin', signifyin', testifyin', and the call and response patterns. The uniqueness of African American culture lies, among other things, in these unique oral traditions that African Americans have been able to develop, use, and disseminate as vehicles for interpretation and communication. This is a hallmark of African American freedom.

Since these various forms of communication are essential to promoting harmony, unity, and solidarity in black relationships that reinforce the power of black communities, we have analyzed and placed them in this category. Let us now turn our attention to celebration as a relational and communal form of freedom.

Praising, Partying, and Celebrating

Other relational and communal forms of freedom are praising, partying, and celebrating. Inherent in black culture and spirituality is the spirit of celebration, where life retains a certain fervor, fire, and joy because of God's goodness in the lives of black people. This spirit of celebration is manifested in every aspect of African American life including culture, religion, music, and the various folkways and mores of black life in general. Celebration and partying are ways in which black people have dissolved the doom and gloom of their existential condition. It is their way of warding off the demons of dehumanization, subjugation, racism, and spiritual terrorism. To celebrate life notwithstanding the trials and troubles of the black experience is to claim psychological and spiritual victory amid the forces of cynicism, terrorism, and despair.

It is utterly amazing that this spirit of partying and celebrating life and God and having a good time can prevail under such difficult circumstances. Seldom do victims of oppression manifest and develop such spirit under conditions of perpetual dehumanization and oppression. Black culture and black spirituality have always stressed the importance of giving God glory, and praying, celebrating, and partying away the troubles of this life.

It is my contention that this is also a dimension of African American freedom that emerges from the practice of black spirituality. The spirit of celebration and joy among black people can never be completely vanquished, and as long as African Americans can find the power to celebrate life and to overcome its troubles and calamities, they can manifest a freedom undashed by the dominant culture.

To sing when there is no real reason to sing and to celebrate life and the power and joy of God notwithstanding a history of slavery, Jim Crow, racial oppression, discrimination, even black-on-black crime and other forms of dehumanization attests to a freedom of the creative and resistant black soul and spirit to transcend the vicissitudes of its condition and surmount the perils of its circumstances.

Any nominal contact with the culture and spirituality of African American people will reveal a certain verve, enthusiasm, and creative energy culminating in various rituals of celebration in African American communities. Again, this is dynamic, creative, and resistant soul force.

Hugging, kissing, singing, reading, praising, laughing, joking, cogitating, shouting, making music and making love, dancing, high and low fiving, rapping, hand clapping, signifying, testifying, and just shooting the breeze are all expressions of black culture, spirituality, and black freedom that are directly inimical to the larger culture. As a rule, white people do not generally conduct themselves in such a celebrative, expressive, "grateful-to-God" mode. Black people celebrate life as a subversion of the wooden, impersonal, staid, nonspiritual, noncelebrative elements of Anglo-American culture.

To sing, shout, dance, and celebrate is not only a therapeutic and medicinal release for black souls on ice but also emblems of opposition to the larger culture with its wooden, archaic patterns of socialization, it methods of devaluation and control, and its multiple forms of domination over black life. To celebrate life is not only good for the soul, but each act of celebration is inherently, if not consciously, a subversion of the values and culture of the status quo. Each expression of joy amid hardship is an act of defiance to the depressive alternations of the larger culture.

Moreover, these various forms of relational and communal celebration were initially developed and cultivated in ceremonies and practices of black spirituality. African American spiritual belief has always emphasized the imperative for black celebration as an emerging and liberating force for African American life. It is the fruit of black soul force, the ultimate manifestation of the liberating power of God in black life and culture. It is here that agony gives out to ecstasy, and joy wins out over unmitigated pain. To celebrate black life is to ultimately confirm, affirm, ritualize, and actualize the supreme power and sovereignty of God in shaping, preserving, and liberating black people from the throes and woes of white racism and despair.

The ultimate symbol of defiance and personal freedom is for black people to quicken the power and spirit of celebration after all the hell they have experienced. This means that the black souls cannot ultimately be sequestered or vanquished and that however mitigating and mutilating their existential circumstances, their bodies, minds, and souls will break free from the chains of servitude and repression. A saving, liberating, and redemptive force in African American community is this undaunted, untrammeled spirit of partying and celebration. We see it robustly manifested in black culture, life, and the ritual practices of the African American church. Understanding the reality of celebration as a force and expression for African American freedom is an important element in fathoming the depth and breadth of the black paradigm of freedom.

Celebration is really a thankfulness and gratitude for the goodness, grace, and power of God's work in the lives of African Americans. To celebrate God and life is to acknowledge the bounteous blessing that God provides each day. To celebrate in community is a collective affirmation of the power of God's love and goodness to work redemptively in black life.

The power to celebrate God manifested in African American spirituality and culture has encouraged and sustained black faith and hope across the years. It has been the seedbed of black sanity and survival, the bedrock of their struggle for dignity and freedom. Celebration thwarts adversity, negates the demons of oppression, and helps African Americans determine their destiny as a people. Without the verve, vitality, joy, and zeal of celebration, black people would have perished years ago in the doldrums of unmitigated depression and despair.

God is a God of life, victory, and celebration, and the essence of black life is having the power to triumphantly celebrate and praise God for the trials they have overcome. At the core of African American spirituality, then, is the power and capacity to claim victory against great odds and allow the spirit to triumph over the calamities of life. Pure, unadulterated joyful praise and celebration of God and life is a hallmark of African American spirituality and freedom.

Five

Spirituality and Cultural Freedom

A consistent theme of this book is the role African American spirituality plays in shaping black consciousness and black culture. The emergence of African American culture can be traced to the genesis of African American spirituality, which had a significant role in developing and sustaining its creative and innovative elements. African American spiritual praxis on plantations in early slave communities created a context and ethos in which the creative ideas and peculiar idioms of African American culture could fully realize themselves and accordingly flourish as socially constructed but spiritually inspired reality. African American spirituality and soul force have always been the primary fount of African American culture, and the latter has had great influence on the subsequent development of black spirituality.

James Haskins and Hugh F. Butts observe:

> Whenever a group of people is accorded a subjugated position in a culture, in order to survive it must band together and form a subculture. Hence, to survive in a culture that has historically ignored them, blacks have had to develop different ways of living, different ways of eating, different ways of dressing, and different modes of speaking, as a kind of code. These different ways of living and speaking evolved in the first place because of blacks' relegation to a subculture.[1]

Accordingly, black creativity in African American culture is not only a salient feature distinguishing it from other cultural forms and idioms but is a catalyst for human freedom. By creating culture, African Americans have established a framework for the practice of human freedom whose creativity sustained itself across three centuries. As long as blacks could create the forms and dynamics of culture, they could preserve a measure of personal autonomy and relative freedom from a system of oppression and domination. In other words, while historically blacks have not been physically, racially, or socially free, they still created a culture of creativity through the praxis of spirituality that allowed them to transcend and overcome the constraints of a dehumanizing and oppressive society.

This is why we have continuously stated throughout this project that African Americans have developed a unique model of freedom. This fact has been sorely overlooked by scholars, activists, and practitioners who repeatedly claim that African Americans are not a free people. While there is much truth in this statement, we must also consider that those thwarting such black freedom are not free either. Here the definitions of freedom are summarily limited to the external Anglo social and political typologies and do not consider the role of black culture and black spirituality in enabling black Americans to develop those internal models of freedom that have invariably accentuated the power of creativity, innovation, and improvisation as principle catalysts for freedom. This means that while black people have been oppressed, they have been free enough to create a culture in which creativity through creative and resistant soul force has been a unifying, transforming, and liberating force for black identity and consciousness in America.

While certain freedoms have historically been denied African Americans, they were able to cultivate a culture and spirituality that encouraged them to create a world in which they could freely interpret and express the meaning of black existence in accordance with their own predilections, powers, and inclinations.

Thus however brutal and repulsive white racism, oppression, and dehumanization, white people could never completely dominate black people because of their capacity to create a culture of expression and innovation that allowed them to negate their full devastation. The uniqueness of the African American paradigm of human freedom, then, lies in the way African American spiritual praxis has cultivated and preserved a culture in which black creativity and creative black soul force have merged to create a matrix and paradigm of human freedom that empowers, transforms, and encourages African American people to realize their optimum potential while keeping their humanity, sanity, and dignity intact. Black people were not allowed to be themselves in the larger society, so they created idioms and nuances of culture that would enable them to find, create, and sustain themselves through the praxis of spirituality and culture. The primary form of human freedom is the freedom to be, and black spirituality and black culture have instilled that in African American people.

Innovation

The freedom to be is directly related to the power to create idioms and elements of culture that preserve and legitimate black identity and existence in America. This has been the unique form of African American freedom in America: the freedom to create a unique culture through spiritual practice and to use that culture as a creative soul force for spiritual and social transformation.

Two important hallmarks of African American culture and spirituality are *innovation* and *improvisation*. Innovation is the power to create something new that either embraces, diverges from, or transcends the normative order or pattern. To innovate is to create a different hermeneutic or motif for human existence. It means taking what is given and transforming it into something meaningful, useful, and purposeful. Innovation suggests the power to see old things in new ways, to forge and create something viable from that which has lost its vitality. African Americans have always been innovative by taking what little they have had and transforming it into something of meaning, power, and value to aid their struggle for human dignity and survival.

Blacks could not have survived without being innovative, without creating something new and vital in a world that had virtually lost all meaning. Innovation is not only manifested in the cultural folkways and mores of black people but also in the walk, talk, styles of dress, culture, music, literature, and food. Howard Paige has provided an insightful analysis of the historical and cultural significance of food in black America.[2] Every aspect of black life exudes some dimensions of innovation that distinguish black culture from other cultural idioms. African Americans have lived innovatively and creatively out of necessity, and possessing the ability to live in such a manner has been a significant element of black freedom in America.

The power of innovation lies not only in the different cultural and folk expressions and creations of black life but also in the development of a black cultural consciousness that has embraced innovation as a creative pattern of cognition and action in the world. Without oversimplifying here, to be African American is not only to act creatively but to think in patterns, configurations, and processes that retain their own elements of creativity, transcendence, and transformation amid virtually constant scrutiny, repression, and opposition. Inherent in black consciousness, culture, and spirituality is the praxis of taking existing reality and translating or transforming it innovatively for constructive purposes. The capacity of black people to do this without the usual amenities and largesse of society is an expression of human freedom because however dire human conditions become, there remains a propensity for innovating life in ways that facilitate black meaning, creativity, and survival.

Without being crass, black people have always taken the leftovers of white folks and used them in ways that created new purpose and vitality for black life. The fact that black people have had to continually if not chronically do this means they have developed a capacity to innovate, to see and interpret and create reality in different ways and on different terms. This capacity to create has virtually been dismissed as the infantile, impulsive, and quixotic personification of a thoughtless and servile people. Everybody knows black people are creative and the power of such creativity, often dismissed as a kind of sycophantic frivolity, has been the source of exploitation of African Americans by hucksters and shysters who have made millions off the ideas and creativity of black folk.

The power of creativity and innovation of black people in America lies in their ability to shape different modes of being, consciousness, and action that embrace but defy the status quo. Innovation is not the hallmark of a people who have no choice but that of a people who can create something meaningful and purposeful for themselves in response to the brutalities and inhumanities of racism and oppression. It is the result of painstaking, thoughtful, advertent, and critical reflection by African Americans to make life purposeful and meaningful.

Innovation is thus an important aspect of black culture and black freedom because it preserves the creativity of pure soul force and invariably ties black people to the wellsprings of personal, spiritual, and cultural vitality. While some black people were not free enough to go to the corner store, they created idioms of life and culture that allowed them to interpret, transcend, and ultimately transform in their own minds, souls, and hearts the pain of not being able to do so.

This is the essence of African American freedom: the power and capacity to create idioms of spirituality, life, and culture that encourage black people freely and innovatively to live with hope, power, and human dignity amid nefarious and formidable conditions. Innovation is the power to think and create on terms that reinforce personal sanctity, identity, and value in a society that has denigrated the creative capacities of African American people.

A great genius of African American people is the manner in which they have appropriated aspects of Anglo culture and synthesized them into a meaningful framework for black existence. Much of the debate about black and white culture simply assumes the Anglo culture has always dictated the terms of amalgamation and enculturation of black people in American society. While this may be true in some measure, it is my belief that black people have retained the freedom to choose those elements of white culture that could innovatively be used and provide meaning to them while simultaneously creating their own culture that reinforced black power, sanity, and survival in American society. Not enough has been written about the genius of black innovation and how the structures, norms, and forms of Anglo culture have been cultivated and developed by blacks for personal empowerment.

This freedom to choose viable aspects of Anglo culture for constructive usage has been obviated or dismissed because of the fallacious view that Anglo culture has had no value or relevance for African Americans. Such views obviate the fact that black people were free or intelligent enough to fathom and filter those subtleties of culture that could be appropriated for their own survival. Both white and black scholars have been guilty of making false assertions about the power and autonomy of African Americans to use the positive and virtuous aspects of Anglo culture for their own survival and the capacity of black people to create a unique culture that synthesizes the best of the Anglo and African traditions. The term "African American" signifies the coalescence of these cultural traditions; the best of Africa, Europe, and America.

We cannot exhaust the various aspects of these cultural proclivities, but suffice to say an important aspect of black cultural freedom is both the way it has appropriated certain aspects of Anglo culture, preserved and redefined the salient aspects of African culture, and wedded these two cultural idioms into a unique matrix and paradigm of creativity and culture that has facilitated their freedom and survival as a people. Innovation has played a large role in enabling black people to develop and devise a unique African American cultural freedom, and we cannot overestimate or downplay its significance.

African American spiritual praxis has always emphasized and encouraged innovation in facilitating black freedom and survival in America through the emergence and preservation of African American creativity and culture. Innovation remains an important construct in the praxis of African American spirituality and culture today.

Improvisation

Another important aspect of African American culture is improvisation. *Improvisation* is a form of innovation but contains the element of spontaneity. Innovation is the result of rational and thoughtful planning or occurs on the moment. Improvisation, while thoughtful, retains elements of creativity and imagination that allow the individual to create something of meaning, power, and value on creative impulse. Impulse is not wild, disordered, and chaotic but the ordered sublimation of creative energies and spontaneity into some meaningful vehicles of reality. It is creative soul force at its best.

African Americans have always had to improvise their existence in America under conditions of uncertainty, terror, and perpetual angst.

Such improvisation has not only compelled blacks to avert the permanent calamities incurred through discrimination, racism, and oppression but has also inspired them to create structures of meaning, value, and purpose amid the vicissitudes of their existential circumstances. To create something of structure and value in a world where dislocation, devaluation, and volatility are extant is the power of improvisation.

In a world where existing structures have had little value or permanence for African Americans, improvisation has been an effective instrument of culture and spirituality, enabling black people to order the chaos and uncertainties of their existence and adeptly navigate through the storms and turbulence of their existential experience.

Improvisation is manifested in every aspect of African American existence. The music, language, folkways, mores, literature, art, and the various ritual dramas, worship, and celebrative ceremonies of African American spiritual praxis all exemplify the spirit of improvisation. Black life itself in America is a form of improvisation, a diversion and divergence from the cognitive, emotive, spiritual, and cultural configurations of white America. Black people have had to improvise to survive. The process of having to improvise has instilled in black people the necessity of doing things differently, of going one step beyond the conventional wisdom and status quo to find power and meaning, of defying and transcending the culture and folkways of white Americans.

Contrary to some belief, improvisation has instilled within black people the imperatives for creating their own configurations and constellations of culture and meaning that do not affirm that black people can only find meaning by insinuating or integrating themselves into the existing structures of their Anglo counterparts. Improvisation means that black people can do new things in new ways. They can embrace existing culture or create their own structures, idioms, and avenues of culture that preserve their sanity, soul, and freedom as a people. The great power of improvisation lies not only in its capacity to transcend the culture of oppression but also in its audacity to improvisationally create new thoroughfares and venues of thought, interpretation, and innovation that give black people new meaning, hope, and spiritual and cultural vitality amid the realities of Anglo culture.

To improvise is to express freedom not as a matter of necessity but as a matter of choice. Black Americans' manifestation and preservation of the gift of improvisation means that they have retained the capacity to stand either within or without Anglo cultural structures to create their own culture of innovation, creativity, and freedom in a society that has enslaved, persecuted, and thoroughly tried to subjugate them.

Thus, oppression and domination of African Americans can never be exhaustive as long as they improvise, which preserves a measure of spiritual and cultural freedom. To improvise is to have the freedom to embrace or transcend, to acknowledge or defy existing values and configurations of Anglo society and culture. This is especially important since culture is often used as an instrument of conquest and domination of various peoples and has played a vital role in the enslavement of Africans who were brought to the new land and whose African deculturation and American enculturation have been the pivotal parentheses of their existence in America.

Yet, improvisation is a cultural retention whose value and role cannot be negated in black freedom in America, for as long as African Americans have improvised in life and culture, they have been able to create and transform those cultural structures of oppression that subvert the various political and social forms of white domination.

An important component of improvisation is *spontaneity*, the capacity to feel, create, and express on the pulse of a moment. This form of cultural freedom has always enabled African Americans to maintain the freedom and autonomy to create works of art according to the entreaties of the spirit soul. Creative soul force again is the form of black spiritual and cultural spontaneity and an important dimension of black spiritual and cultural freedom.

Creative Black Soul Force and the Black Culture Soul

Innovation and improvisation find their roots in the black soul force and the black culture soul that we previously cited. While other cultures use innovation and improvisation as distinguishing elements of culture in relation to a culture of oppression, a distinguishing feature of African American culture is the role of black soul force in shaping the black culture soul. *Black soul force* is a parental source of African American spirituality and culture. The activation of black soul force as a bastion of cultural and spiritual freedom of African Americans has led to the formation of a black culture soul.

Hence, we cannot fathom black culture without the informing, unifying, and transforming dimensions of black soul force. Soul force is an integral aspect of black culture. Thus we have the *black culture soul,* which creates, cultivates, and sustains through the praxis of black culture and spirituality those archives and lexicons of black belief, ritual, value, and custom that facilitate and reinforce black solidarity and freedom. Black soul force is the undergirding dynamic of black solidarity, transformation, and liberation. The black culture soul establishes those archival structures of culture that reinforce value, legitimacy, and meaning in black life.

   The fundamental reality distinguishing African American culture as a unifying and liberating dynamic of black freedom is black soul force. It is the raw material and sacred substance of African American spirituality. It provides black people with power, joy, and resiliency, the creative energy and vitality to transform the brutalities of existence into positive realities of grace, wholeness, and healing. It translates the absurdities of black life into a language of redemption, love, and liberation, and compels black people to transcend those insurmountable social, political, racial, and relational barriers to black positivity and freedom that obstruct and stymie the self and collective realization of their optimum power and potential.

   Black soul force is the seedbed and parental source of black consciousness, culture, and spirituality and is the overriding reality to the absurdities and calamities of black existence. The rhythms, unity, and power of black soul force constitute the positive dynamics of black culture and spirituality. Without creative and resistant soul force, black people could not create a dynamic culture of spirituality that has sustained their freedom as an oppressed people in America. Thus sorrow is turned into joy, misfortune into prosperity, and despair into hope.

   Moreover, it is the power of black soul force that has enabled black people to develop their own spirituality and culture of freedom and compelled them to live innovatively, improvisationally, and positively amid the realities of oppression and dehumanization. More than any other force of black life, black soul force, as rooted in the power and reality of God, has instilled within black people a will, capacity, and proclivity to thwart their full, unmitigated dehumanization and domination as a people. The expression of soul force in black life is the manifestation of black souls, minds, and hearts breaking free from the constraints, conventions, and oppressive codes of Anglo-American society in ways and forms that exemplify and reinforce the transformative reality of black humanity, spirituality, and vitality.

   The practice, presence, and power of soul force of African Americans in the creation and perpetuation of culture and spirituality would never allow black Americans to completely comply with their own subjugation by white people or any other people. The great value of African American spirituality has been the positive ritual nurturing of black soul force as a hallmark of black life and culture. It has been the continual practice of African American spirituality in black life that has allowed soul force to flourish as an important dimension of African American existence.

   We see the use of soul force in every area of black life, whether it is musicians creating and singing music, preachers delivering sermons, or black mothers and fathers raising their children and instilling in them the values of love, self-respect, and human dignity. It all results from belief in a loving, caring, and redeeming God. It is a manifestation of positive spiritual teachings, the power of the soul to inform, create, and cultivate human wholeness and positive transformation. Soul force is the essential element of black culture and black spirituality. It is the foundation of black creativity and the central catalyst enabling black people to surmount and overcome the trials and terrors of black existence. It is the basis of African American freedom.

Soul force equally actualizes faith and hope so that there is no condition, circumstance, or situation that African Americans have not been able to confront and vanquish. If the power of the soul equipped African Americans to survive four centuries of racism, oppression, discrimination, and dehumanization without losing their dignity, self-respect, and the ability to create a meaningful culture and spirituality that actualizes black freedom, it is the most vital force in African American life.

Soul is not only the black lifeline to God but also the source of invention and creativity in black culture and black spirituality. It is the quintessential substance and élan of African American existence. Without soul force, black people could not have survived slavery, Jim Crow, centuries of oppression, dehumanization, and dislocation without losing their own souls in the doldrums of despair.

Without soul force black people could not have created spirituals, the blues, jazz, rap, gospel, reggae, and rock and roll. Without soul force the black church could not have survived, black preaching would not be as powerful and efficacious in moving black souls toward positive personal and social transformation. Soul force and the black culture soul are two of the most important elements distinguishing African American culture from other cultures and idioms. The foundation of black freedom, it is the definitive factor shaping the life, vitality, and destiny of African American people.

Soul force is synonymous with black life, culture, and spirituality. It is unmistakably and inseparably tied to black consciousness, creativity, and identity and culminates in black spiritual and social empowerment.

Black Music

We have stated that the culture of African Americans has been a vital force for freedom. Black music has been a central catalyst in facilitating black freedom and remains an important reality in black life today. Music

issuing from the dregs of the soul of black life has had a profound impact
on black people's understanding of themselves and has fostered a unique
black identity in the culture of the American experience.

Black music has harmonized the chaos of black life, empowered black
people to surmount the perils of oppression through creativity, and
vaulted them over the cultural constraints of their overlords who reinforce and value black servitude, devaluation, and subjugation.

In Africa, one of the important founts of African American music, musicians played music to rally the community for some common purpose,
to harmonize the chaos and uncertainties of life, and to prepare warriors
for battle.

African American music has been a force for liberation and change for
black people in America and perhaps more than any other idiom in black
culture captures the essence of black soul force and the larger culture soul.
John Miller Chernof describes the music of Africa as follows:

> In music, the contrasting, tightly organized rhythms are power-
> ful—powerful because there is vitality in rhythmic conflict, pow-
> erful precisely because people are affected and moved. As people
> participate in a musical situation, they mediate the conflict, and
> their immediate presence gives power a personal form so that
> they may relate to it.[3]

In discussing the role of music in African communal life, J. H. Kwabena
Nketia observes: "Sometimes the schedule of musical activities is related
to the beliefs of a community—to the wishes of the gods they worship or
to the reactions evoked from the spirits and forces that are believed to play
a vital role in the drama of human existence."[4] Leroi Jones states that black
music has a vital function in maintaining a distinct black identity among
the masses. This music has not been "appropriated" by the black and
white middle classes so as to obscure its roots and distinctiveness as a cultural and social reality.[5]

Differentiating the function of Western and African music, Francis Bebey
says: "Westerners are frequently at a loss to understand the music of black
Africa: the concepts of Africans are so totally different. African musicians
do not seek to combine sounds in a manner pleasing to the ear. Their aim is
simply to express life in all of its aspects through the medium of sound."[6]

Both African and African American music are powerful cultural entities shaping the form and trajectory of black communal life, and any serious study of black music must consider these salient dimensions of the
black music as an art form and force for spiritual and cultural liberation.
Let us then turn our attention to the predominant forms of black music in
African American life and culture.

The Spirituals

James Cone and Howard Thurman have done fine work in exploring the eschatological and liberating dimensions of the spirituals.[7] Eileen Southern has provided a comprehensive examination of the history of black music in America,[8] and recently Jon Michael Spencer has offered a penetrating analysis of the liberation motifs in black sacred music.[9]

A central theme of the spirituals is liberation. Created as a musical form in slavery, this music spoke to the upward longing of black people to be liberated from the dregs of persecution and oppression.

> Go down, Moses,
>   and tell Ole Pharaoh,
> "Let my people go."

> Deep river,
>   I long to cross over into camp ground.

In the development of the spirituals, black music not only became an instrument of spiritual freedom and cultural liberation but also a litany of hope for God's acts in history. The music not only spoke of black life, death, liberation, and transformation but also invoked God's miraculous intervention in history in much the same way that God intervened for the Hebrews in Egypt.

The important thing to remember about the spirituals is not only the creative and resourceful wellspring of spirituality that watered their roots but also the use of culture and spirituality as a means of freeing black souls from the onus of daily oppression. The spirituals emerged from the rich oasis of black soul force, and the practice and development of black spirituality created the context in which such creativity could flourish under conditions of discrimination and oppression.

This means that slaves had developed a vital and meaningful relationship with God where the troubles of this world would soon be overcome as an actual historical event. Important here to remember is not only the theme of liberation and transformation manifested in the spirituals but also the power of such music to shape consciousness, behavior, identity, and culture amid dehumanizing and oppressive conditions.

We can scarce conceive of the spirituals without considering the role of black spirituality in shaping and influencing their formation and preservation as a unique art form. That African American spirituality has been a integral element in impacting the music and culture of black Americans cannot be disputed, for it was on the slave ships, around the camp fires and hush harbors on plantations that black souls first expressed their deeper longings and yearnings for meaning, power, and purpose in the spirituals as they lived under the terror of their white masters.

> O freedom! O freedom!
> O freedom over me!
> An' befo' I'd be a slave,
> I'll be buried in my grave,
> An' go home to my Lord an' be free.

We stated earlier that black music has historically helped shape the chaos of black life and provided a very intelligent, if not deceptive, way to codify black power and aspirations. A central thesis of this book is that it is in the very creation of black music—in the spirituals, jazz, the blues, and other musical forms—black people are expressing spiritual and cultural freedom as a means of embracing but subverting the brutalities and de-humanization of the dominant culture of oppression.

In regard to the spirituals, conventional wisdom and interpretation have invariably posited that the music itself expresses a deeper longing for black freedom, that the content of the spirituals delineated a desire of slaves to escape slavery either through physical death or by running away from the plantation. While this is true, something often overlooked is the fact that for black people to create this kind of music expressing freedom and liberation was itself an act of freedom. This required not only pro-found mind but resilient spirit!

Again, we corroborate a central thesis of this work: that social and po-litical freedom were only two of the types of freedom that black slaves sought. However, their social and political enslavement did not thwart the creation of cultural and spiritual freedom that served as catalysts for their psychospiritual liberation. That the spirituals were even created at all under such horrendous and heinous conditions attests to the cultural and spiritual freedom of African Americans. While their bodies were not free, their minds, spirits, souls, and hearts were free enough to fashion a culture, an ethos and a reality that simulated culturally and spiritually what they could not achieve socially and politically. The creation of the spirituals is a hallmark of the African American paradigm of freedom not simply because of the inherent themes of freedom but also because they were creatively fashioned from the best of Anglo and African culture and developed under conditions of extreme subjugation and oppression.

James Cone has done some of the most definitive work on the liberat-ing aspects of the spirituals. Henry Mitchell, Gayraud Wilmore, and Theo Witvliet have all offered important analyses of the survival and liberation themes in black spirituals.[10] An equally important work is Joseph R. Washington, Jr.'s book *Black Religion,* in which he observes:

The dignity, beauty, insight, and classic quality of the spirituals as the creative contribution of the Negro to the world is a matter of record. They are most significant when placed against the background of insurrections, protracted camp meetings, religious festivities, moral exhortations, and the urge for freedom planted by the free Negro. . . . As an expression of religion, rather than of faith, some Negro spirituals were songs of protest, in acceptable and thinly veiled form, against the conditions of this life. As such, they were songs of defiance, revolt, and escape.[11]

While these black scholars address liberation as manifested in both the content and function of black spirituals, few have spoken to the issue of how their very conceptualization and creation exemplify a cultural and spiritual freedom in itself. The fact that this unique artistic idiom was created by a socially and racially oppressed people means that they possessed in their hearts, minds, and souls a creative and spiritual freedom that lifted them beyond the veil of oppression.

The primary presuppositions of black freedom are invariably rooted in Anglo cultural model and norms, which address freedom only in its social and political forms and not its cultural and spiritual dimensions. It is precisely my argument that the African American paradigm of freedom addresses the freedom of spirit, mind, and soul as they confront and overcome the social, external conditions of oppression and captivity and that black spirituality and black culture have invariably functioned as a force for freedom in this regard. While the spirituals speak to the concern for human freedom, their very creation is a manifestation of an internal freedom of mind and soul that is often obviated in favor of those external social and political forms of freedom that blacks have so assiduously sought to achieve.

Black spirituality not only created the refuge and context in which the spirituals as a creative idiom of black music were to emerge but provided the theological basis of liberation, transformation, and hopeful expectation about God's eschatological intervention in the continuum of human history. Unwavering belief in a God of change and freedom helped black people preserve an autonomy of soul, spirit, and mind that compelled them to create the spirituals not only as an expression but also as an act of freedom under conditions of oppression.

In the stress on the exigencies and urgencies of social and political freedom, scholars and activists have often omitted the ways in which black culture and black spirituality have functioned as a vital force for liberation and transformation in African American life. That the spirituals *were created* is a powerful and creative manifestation of a people who have not been completely and summarily subjugated and destroyed by the culture of their oppressors.

By actualizing creative and resistant soul force, improvisation, and innovation, African Americans retained an interior freedom of mind, soul, and spirit that compelled them to create a culture of the soul that ultimately conferred on them meaning, purpose, and vitality in a world that consistently tried to dislocate and alienate them. Those who are socially and politically free have not always been so culturally and spiritually free so as to create unique paradigms and idioms of music that are native to the American context. Howard Thurman makes in his discussion of the spirituals the following observation about human creative propensities:

> Every man recognizes that he is a creature with a body, a face, a mind; and at the same time there is something in him that always wants to fly. There is something in every one of us that tries ever to reach beyond the known, the realized, the given, the particular. The struggle seems never to be resolved; man, the earth-bound creature, with his mind and spirit moving in and out among the stars. Such is the gothic principle in human life.[12]

Thus the spirituals not only discuss black people's need and desire to "fly" in Thurman's terms but are also a manifestation of a people already in spiritual and cultural flight from dehumanizing and subjugating conditions.

African American spirituality as a force for transformation and liberation has highly influenced the cultivation of spirituals through the following emphases. It has cultivated and instilled in black people the imperative for establishing a living relationship with a transcendent and liberating God. Second, it has developed those interior creative resources of mind, soul, imagination, and spirit that equip black people with the resiliency and tenacity to exceed the constraints, barriers, and impediments created by racism, oppression, and various processes of domestication. Third, it has developed and actualized those resources, powers, and potential that facilitate the realization of optimum potential both individually and collectively among black people. African American spirituality has thus created a context where the content, structure, dynamic, and forms of creative culture and spirituality have been allowed to emerge as a force for empowerment and liberation for African Americans under conditions where external social and political forms of freedom were largely denied them. Thus spirituals bear witness to the resourcefulness, power, and vitality of African American spirituality as a catalyst for black spiritual and cultural freedom.

Gospel Music

A more recent extension of spirituals and blues (discussed below) themes have culminated in the creation of gospel music. While the ideas of freedom and liberation are less manifest in the lyrics of gospel music, it demonstrates the power of creative soul force as an instrument of black spirituality and culture. The creativity of gospel music is largely disclosed in the structures, forms, and styles of the music itself. While liberation may not be a salient theme, one expression of the music itself exemplifies the freedom of creativity and soul force optimizing the best of African American spiritual and cultural traditions. The creation of gospels as a genre of music also attests to the freedom inherent in black culture and black spirituality.

The Blues

James Cone provides an insightful description of the blues:

> The blues depict the "secular" dimension of black experience. They are "worldly" songs which tell us about love and sex, and about that other "mule kickin' in my stall." They tell us about the "Black Cat's Bones," "a Mojo hand," and "dese backbitin' womens tryin' fo' to steal my man." The blues are about black life and the sheer earth and gut capacity to survive in an extreme situation of oppression. Black music, then, is not an artistic creation for its own sake; rather it tells us about the *feeling* and *thinking* of African people, and the kinds of mental adjustments they had to make in order to survive in an alien land.[13]

For Cone, the blues are a kind of secular spiritual that reflect the power of black adaptation for survival in America. Leroi Jones contends that the blues are really a manifestation of those elements of black life that more refined blacks have repudiated in order not to identify with their African roots.[14] Samuel Charters delineates the similarities of African American blues and African folk songs.[15]

Whatever the view, the blues have functioned as music not only lamenting the sometimes deplorable state of black existence but also as a kind of ridicule commentary on the absurdities of love and trouble in black life. The blues are really a form of musical signifying that not only display a defiance against the polite conventions of society and its customs but create their own revolutionary pattern of construction and interpretation that dismiss the absurd as absurd. The blues call life like it is and arrive at direction through various means of indirection. John Lee

Hooker says, "Suffer, Suffer, Suffer, ain't gonna suffer no more." Albert Collins talks about catching his lover in an affair because he recognizes there is a problem when there are "too many dirty dishes when I come home from work."

Slavery, as Cone and Jones have observed, is the background from which the blues emerge as a secular musical form. The blues contain a black funk, a nitty-gritty, down-home quality that embodies the soul and sensibility of African American people. The fact that a person who has been done wrong by his lover can create the music itself is a thorough expression of human freedom. One is therefore not so far down in the dumps that he or she cannot set his or her troubles into meaningful music. The power of God and the Spirit is to free the oppressed to sing "anyhow."

The blues then are an expression of human freedom, for the creation of this unique art form helps to chase the blues away. James Cone is again helpful: "For example, the work songs were a means of heightening energy, converting labor into dances and games, and providing emotional excitement in an otherwise unbearable situation. The emphasis was on free, continuous, creative energy as produced in song."[16] Freedom is expressed in the creative energy providing the emotional and spiritual release from the pain and suffering of life. The blues are also a kind of secular narrative on the power of the artist to overcome, outsmart, or outdo adversaries. Just as the spirituals speak of freedom from "ole massa"* and pharaoh, the blues delineate the capacity of the downhearted and dejected to surmount the troubles and trials of human experience. While the lyrics of blues often provide a plaintive lament about being done wrong by somebody or something, they also provide a medium and idioms of relief from the emotional and relational tyrannies of life in general.

The spiritual implications of many blues ballads allude to the singer's virtual miraculous or divine capacity to know "something ain't right" or intuit some trouble on the horizon. In this sense the blues are not only a plaintive expression of sorrow but are also created to chart safe passage through the storms of life. While very few references are made to divine intervention in the blues, an undergirding theme is the capacity of the jilted lover or the betrayed spouse who finds solace and triumph through some higher spiritual power or resource. The freedom of blues as a musical art form in black life resides in the capacity of the emotionally and relationally oppressed to fashion an idiom of communication and creativity that actualizes a capacity to overcome the struggles of this life. The blues inherently provide a commentary on the strength of black people to inter-

---

*Ole massa is a term that was used by black slaves to describe their white masters.

pret, name, confront, and overcome the adversities and calamities of their human condition.

We cannot overestimate the role of freedom that helps to create the blues as well as spirituals. The creative and dynamic energies that inform and enhance the cultivation of the blues as an art form cannot be negated, for they are equally a manifestation of black soul force where the individual demonstrates the capacity to turn sorrow into joy and defeat into victory. This is a prominent theme in African American spiritual belief systems and can be seen in the blues as well as in other black musical genres. Thus freedom is manifested not only in the capacity of black people to create the blues, tell a story, and claim a victory but also in the ability of the music to reveal intrinsically if not overtly, themes that dramatize a recurring theme promulgated in African American spiritual belief systems and that is the capacity of the human spirit to heal and mend, to surmount and soar under conditions of brokenness, pain, and alienation.

Jon Michael Spencer has done definitive work in this area by citing "theodicies" of the blues: "Like all theodicies, the theodicies of the blues are fundamentally historic because they comprise a synthesis of (1) the personal narrative reflections of blues singers, (2) historical reality that evidences the problem of evil and suffering, and (3) biblical narratives learned during bluespeople's upbringing in the church."[17] The blues are really a secular testimony to the resiliency of the human spirit to face, confront, and overcome the pain of adversity. What could be more spiritual than this? This is a salient theme in African American spirituality, and because God gives the oppressed the ability to triumph, freedom is actualized in the movement and power of the Spirit to transform lives. Spencer also delineates the element of "reaping what you sow" in the blues, which also has divine implications.[18]

It is equally significant that blacks have had the freedom to create a music that emanates from the concerns of the soul but whose reach has much broader tentacles in speaking to ultimate concerns of black existence. Although the blues are a kind of secular music, they are not devoid of sacred emphases or spiritual and divine inferences. Freedom here is actualized in the power of the music to speak to a multiplicity of concerns—both sacred and secular—in black life, and this could be achieved because in African American culture, as in African culture, the lines between them are not highly differentiated. John Michael Spencer again observes:

> Restoring wholeness and balance in the lives of the disinherited is the work of the "blues god," as evidenced by the success blues has had in synthesizing the sacred and the secular. In this respect the performances of Bessie Smith evoked the mood and fervor of

southern black worship. "She was real close to God, very religious," recalls one of her musicians. "She always mentioned the
Lord's name. That's why her blues seemed almost like hymns."[19]

This freedom to move across boundaries and barriers in the art form itself
is also emblematic of the freedom of black people to exceed the constraints
and parameters defined for them by the larger culture. In Anglo culture
the demarcations between sacred and secular are highly differentiated. In
African American life the divisions are not so salient, if they exist at all.

This freedom to envision everything as part of a continuous whole, as an
integral part of one universe is a significant presupposition of African and
African American spirituality. The capacity to transcend the boundaries
and barriers of the white culture and society is the quintessence of the
African American paradigm of freedom. Thus, freedom is not simply having the capacity to go where one pleases socially or geographically but
also the ability to go beyond the cultural, spiritual, and creative nomen-
clatures and spheres considered off limits by the larger white society. To
intrude on the conventions of the dominant culture musically and culturally is an act of freedom socially and politically. That blues musicians can
combine sacred and secular themes with no problem is emblematic of
black cultural and spiritual freedom.

Without being redundant, we must again affirm this spirit, power, or
capacity as one of the most significant aspects of African American freedom. Black people have always possessed an intrinsic ability to defy and
transcend the conventions and customs of white people in this society. We
see this tendency manifested in the creation of spirituals, the blues, jazz,
gospel, and other forms of African American music.

This capacity to creatively extend beyond the barriers and taxonomies
of white society has been instilled in African American spiritual praxis,
for blacks have always looked to a transcendent, transforming, and liberating God as a foundation for black existence in America. Such spiritual
belief is the axis of black life, identity, and culture in America. The blues,
like the spirituals, issue from creative black soul force that invariably
seeks to break free from the constraints, dogmas, and oppressive structures of white society and convention. As long as black people can create
the blues as a funky, folksy art form, freedom of the spirit through black
soul force will be continually preserved.

Jazz (American "Classical" Music)

Another important medium of black music that is also an emblem of
freedom emerging from black spirituality is jazz, otherwise known as
American classical music. Classical music has been defined as anything

transcending its origins, and jazz has achieved such status. It is embraced around the world as a thoughtful, creative, and innovative music. Margaret Just Butcher says, "Classical jazz is an important part of typical or national American music and must be evaluated as one the Negro's major cultural contributions."[20]

The structures and configurations of jazz demonstrate African American creativity at its best. Intelligence, creativity, innovation, improvisation, and structure are all benchmarks of this unique musical genre. The creation of jazz itself is a manifestation of different cognitive processes that culminate in the formation of a musical hermeneutic that is entrepreneurial, dashing, and highly unconventional. That jazz has been created as an American art form sui generis attests to the power and freedom of black people to culturally and spiritually create their own language and hermeneutic of existence that embraces but transcends the cultural status quo.

Jazz coalesces the best of European and African musical traditions. It emerged from the black church. Critics of Ralph Ellison's work describe him as writing in the rhythms of jazz culture. Leroi Jones has discussed jazz's power and influence on black life in America.[21] The power of jazz lies not only in its creativity, structure, and longevity but also in its liberating and transforming power to change African American life. There is a notion of thinking and conceptualizing, doing and acting in jazz motifs. Inherent in black life is not only a poetry of motion and thought but also the capacity to respond to reality in improvisational forms of creativity and vitality that empower black people. The power lies not only in the form, rhythm, and beat but also in the creative and improvisational structures, the techniques of black life and culture that enable black people to confront, transform, and transcend their condition through the implements of culture.

Thus, while the revolutionary fervor of black life may not have always been actualized through political and social processes, the true and permanent revolution has occurred through black culture and black spirituality; through the creation of those cognitive, cultural, ontological, and spiritual configurations that give black people a unique identity and equip them to face, confront, and ultimately transcend their condition and plight. The revolt of black people then culminates in the creation of a spirituality of culture and a culture of spirituality wherein creativity, improvisation, innovation, and structural transformation create an ethos of sanity, healing, transformation, and wholeness amid the constraints and debilitations of African American life in America.

We stated earlier that jazz emerged from the bosom of the black church. Part of this is based on the call and response pattern of jazz music. Kathy

J. Ogren alludes to this in the following description of jazz improvisation: "One important early source of improvisation was the 'call and response' tradition of Afro-American sacred and secular music, in which musical ideas developed out of exchanges between a leader and chorus. This process encourages audience participation in the creation of music."[22] The problem is that it was defined as the devil's music by people within and without the church, which negated its intrinsic value as an art form. Because jazz was forced underground and played in brothels and other nocturnal environs where sinners gathered and defiled their souls, it was denigrated as the devil's music. Ogren also tells us:

> Jazz was obviously a music in which blacks were the primary creators and whites often the imitators. Black and white musicians generally did not play in the same ensembles during jazz's formative years, although performers often heard each other's performances. Equally obvious, jazz was a music of raw emotions— of hard luck and of good times, of lust and loneliness. At first, neither jazz nor the places where it was played fell under the control of respectable whites. The morally and culturally subversive aspects of jazz stirred anxieties that fueled a long-running public controversy in the 1920s.[23]

Elsewhere Ogren states:

> Black Americans debated the character of their music and musical performance long before the jazz controversy of the 1920s began. The issues were rooted in the evolution of music during slavery. Although much of the music on the plantation was sacred, secular music such as work songs, dance songs, sacrificial songs, and ballads made up a significant portion of slave music. Slave musicians developed their skills in religious worship and as performers for both their masters and the slave community. Opposition to some music, especially fiddle tunes and blues developed because of bawdy lyrics and the secular themes of some songs. Since the antiphonal forms of Afro-American sacred and secular music are quite similar, it was not primarily differences in song structure that differentiated respectable from disreputable music: it was performance context and lyrics.[24]

While one might understand how jazz acquired the "devil's music" label, such nomenclature obviates the significance and power of jazz as an art form. In order to survive in America, black people had to live in jazz idioms and forms as a means of polite and often vehement defiance of white culture and the white establishment. From swing to bebop from free jazz to fusion—they all signify the freedom of a people to live and create, to think and act in ways that defy and transcend cultural convention.

Musically speaking, jazz has always been the music of freedom, the apex of black cultural and spiritual creativity. While black people were not always politically or socially free, they were free to create a unique culture and spirituality that embodied all the values, aspirations, presuppositions, and dispositions of socially and politically free people. The culture and spirituality of African Americans has provided a freedom of the mind, heart, and soul that even their oppressors, who have been presumably free all along, have not embodied or exemplified in the American experience.

That jazz has been created is an expression of a culturally free people. That jazz is still being created means that such freedom lives on in the hearts and minds of its creators. Ogren is again helpful here:

> The most important "ways of speaking" in jazz were shaped by musical traditions that relied on significant interactions between performers and audiences. This exchange encouraged spontaneity and culminated in the defining features of jazz: improvisation, call and response techniques, polyrhythms, syncopation, and blue tonalities.[25]

At the heart of jazz is the gift of improvisation that Ogren helps to clarify: "Improvisation is perhaps the best-known musical element in jazz. All musical creativity develops, at least in part, because composers or performers alter the rhythmic, harmonic, or melodic ideas of musicians who preceded them. Improvisation is central to all jazz performance."[26] Marshall Stearns describes the six differentiating factors of jazz that have strong affinities with African American spiritual traditions: rhythm, blue tonality, the call and response pattern, allusion songs, ring shout, and falsetto break.[27]

Another important aspect of jazz as with all black music is the rhythmic dimensions and the role of the bass as an underlying pulse to the movement of the music. In traditional West African music the bass and drum are the driving voices and forces of the music. The music moves and grooves on the floatations and flirtations of bass and drum. Sule Greg Wilson and Ashenafi Kebede provide important analysis of the role of these instruments in African and African American music.[28] This is especially true in jazz.

Improvisation, polyrhythmic configurations, and spiritual pulsations are benchmarks of the music. The emergence of jazz as an art form exemplifies the vitality, dexterity, and profundity of African American spirituality and culture.

Jazz is the music of freedom, the soul of African Americana. Perhaps more than any other music in the history of African Americans, it describes and defines every condition, embraces the sacred and secular, speaks to mind and soul, moves body and being into other realms of contemplation and existence. The experience of jazz is not only cerebral but ethereal. It amalgamates the best of European classical music with the syncopations of black rhythms and culture while creating new paradigms of communication in distinctive musical modalities.[29]

We cannot say enough about jazz. It has often been frivolously and summarily dismissed as asymmetrical, infantile, and incongruous with European classical music. However, many of the jazz giants, such as Miles Davis, Charlie Parker, and John Coltrane, studied the European classical composers as a means of strengthening jazz in their search for new musical ideas. The tragedy is that many black jazz musicians have had to go abroad to receive just dues for their art. Jazz appears to be more celebrated and acclaimed in Europe and other parts of the world than in the American homeland that gave it birth. Fortunately, in some sectors of America, jazz is experiencing a resurgence among younger people.

The point here is that jazz is one of the most creative forces in African American life. As with all black music, it has not only helped to shape the chaos and vicissitudes of black life in America but has also provided a voice, a medium of articulation for the hopes, dreams, aspirations, and interpretations of blackness in America. Jazz is the soul of America and speaks fervently and religiously to those matters of the mind, body, and soul that are ultimate concerns of black life.

In *Street Corner Theology,* the following observation about Charlie "Yardbird" Parker is made:

> Transcendence, exaltation, freedom of expression, and lived prosperity, however fleeting and ephemeral, were watchwords of countless numbers of African Americans. As spokesperson of the masses, his musical vocabulary was replete with such terminology, and he said with his horn what others could not say with their tongues. He spoke to their dreams. He spoke to their souls. This had to be God, very God, revolutionizing a people through a black bopper from Kansas City.[30]

Liberation through music is a central objective of jazz. Not only do the structures of the art personify a new musical paradigm, but improvisation as a central vehicle of the art epitomizes the reality of freedom.[31]

We stated earlier that the creation of jazz is a product of African American culture and spirituality. The congruities of jazz with black spirituality are not only found in their structures and modalities, such as call and response and blue tonality, but also in the function of the music as a kind of liberating soul force from the constraints of white culture and society.

More than any other music, jazz symbolizes the freedom, creativity, genius, and vitality of African American people. Black spirituality as the creative fount of black life and culture has been the central source of black creativity and black music. Wyatt T. Walker is correct when he says that music expresses the soul of a people and reflects how and what they are thinking at a given time in history.[32]

Because of the liberating aspects of jazz as music and as a bona fide hermeneutic of black existence, we cannot underplay its role in shaping the consciousness and aspirations of black people in America. The music was created as an expression of black creativity and cultural freedom and its message, structures, and dynamics exemplify the continual struggle of the human spirit and soul to break free from the restraints that bind, oppress, and ultimately destroy its sense of wholeness and vitality. That jazz remains the only indigenous musical art form in America affirms not only its substance but also its power to speak over the broad expanse of American cultural history. The soul force of black spirituality is the soul force of jazz and other forms of black music in America.

European Classical Music

Classical music is not foreign to the African American experience. Many black people have studied classical music and numerous black composers have made significant contributions to the art form. Edward Jones reminds us that some of the great European classical composers were of African descent, including Ludwig von Beethoven, Franz Joseph Haydn, and Wolfgang Amadeus Mozart.[33]

We stated earlier an essential element of the African American paradigm of freedom is evidenced in the way black Americans have appropriated the positive aspects of Anglo-American culture and wedded them with extant Africanisms to create a unique African American culture. This means that African American culture is not a negation of Euro-American cultural forms for the sake of identifying with and preserving the African but a coalescence of the best of both realities. Charles Adams put it this way:

> European Americans and African Americans have helped to create each other. We are simultaneously baroque and impressionistic, classical and modern, European and African. . . . A glance at the Egyptian pyramids reveals that African culture is not totally spontaneous. Likewise, an evening of Italian grand opera is enough evidence that emotionalism is not a stranger to European experience.[34]

The political realities of white racism, oppression, subjugation, and deculturalization of black people have done much to obviate and obscure those positive aspects of Euro-American culture that black people have adopted for their own survival and edification. The assumption here is that all aspects of Euro-American culture are reprehensible, which is a misconstruction, and that black people, because of racism and oppression, were not free or intelligent enough to create a culture that ingeniously fused the culture of their captors with their own African retentions.

An additional assumption is that black people have been coerced into adopting the virtues of white culture because they had no choice, or if the choices were consciously made, it was because they have inferiorized their own culture in order to identify with that of whites. While some of this may be true, as E. Franklin Frazier and Nathan Hare have observed, there remains a remnant of black people whose choices were made not because of a feeling of cultural inferiority or fear of rejection by whites but because they were free and fearless enough in their thinking to understand that all cultures have positive aspects, even the culture of the oppressor.[35] It is African American spirituality that has inherently instilled within black people the propensity for embracing the positive aspects of reality while transcending its corruptions.

Many of the great classical musicians and performers received their start in music in the black church because the church has always affirmed the positive dimensions of culture and art as forms of personal and collective empowerment. Many of the black classical musicians emerging from the black church embraced European classical music because it resonated with their being and soul and motivated them to develop their gifts for the glory of God. Paul Robeson, Theodore Jones, Marian Anderson, Kathleen Battle, Barbara Hendricks, Roland Hayes, Jessie Norman, George Shirley, William Warfield, William Grant Still, and many others received their inspiration from the black church and African American spiritual teachings.

Black spirituality has not only instilled within black people a tenacity and resiliency against all forms of subjugation and oppression but has equally inculcated within them a standard of excellence and appreciation for culture as a creative force for education, empowerment, and change. African American spirituality has always taught the imperatives for embracing that which is positive and transcending that which is negative or destructive. We see this tendency manifested in various aspects of African American life and culture.

Contrary to widespread myopia and ignorance, many black classical musicians have not appropriated the music in order to be *white* but to explore a musical realm that could cultivate the best and highest in them as persons seeking to hone their artistic gifts. The same is true for jazz, blues, ragtime, and other forms of African American music. Black people have used music as a cultural force for freedom in the world. The fact that

African Americans have been freely able to embrace European classical music as well as to develop their own musical paradigms in jazz and blues exemplifies the power of soul force as an instrument of freedom in black life. The freedom to embrace existing traditions or develop a tradition uniquely African American is highly influenced by African American spiritual praxis and belief. This epitomizes the meaning of the African American model of freedom: the power to adopt, adapt, synthesize, cultivate, and transform a hermeneutics and paradigm of survival and empowerment that enable black people to live with dignity and realize human wholeness and actualize their optimum potential.

Black Folktales and Literature

J. Mason Brewer, Langston Hughes, Arna Bontemps, and others have done outstanding work in preserving, editing, and interpreting the various aspects of black folklore and other literature.[36] A significant aspect of black folktales and literature, particularly in the Brer Rabbit stories and other tales, is the capacity of the proponent to outsmart and outwit his opponents. Numerous themes pervade African American literature from its genesis to the present, but a predominant motif is the ability of the underdog to overcome or transcend barriers through personal ingenuity and resourcefulness that baffles his adversaries.

Survival, intelligence, ingenuity, and creativity are themes that repeatedly manifest themselves in the literature of African Americans. The oral preponderance of black culture also has been preserved in black literature and rappin', signifyin', and testifyin' of which we spoke earlier are highly salient.

The power of freedom for African Americans is embodied in the spoken as well as the written word and numerous writers have used their pens as instruments of freedom and transformation in African American life. Whether the poetry of Phillis Wheatley, Maya Angelou, or Langston Hughes, the prose of James Baldwin, Richard Wright, Zora Neale Hurstone, or Leon Forrest, the plays of Ed Bullins, Robert Douglas, Lorraine Hansberry, or August Wilson—the themes of personal freedom and spirituality, the realization of collective humanity and opportunity amid untoward and sometimes desolate circumstances always shine through.

African American literature has invariably delineated the necessity for black people to celebrate their own humanity, preserve their own identity, and actualize freedom in the midst of racism and oppression. But more important, in much of these writings we see the preservation and articulation of creative soul force, a force that speaks eloquently, defiantly, and sometimes patiently from the deeper recesses of the human mind and spirit. It is a spirit that exhorts African Americans to realize and celebrate every fiber and iota of their humanity in their quest for wholeness and fulfillment.

Bernard W. Bell, Gayl Jones, Addison Gayle, Jr., Larry Neal, Henry Louis Gates, Jr., and others have spoken well to the salient themes of African American literature.[37] Freedom of mind, body, and soul continue to be prominent issues in African American literature. The recent emergence of black women writers also reveals the necessities of freedom from oppression by black men. Here the question of bondage is not only mind but soul, heart, and spirit, and in many cases are black on black instead white on black. The oppressive and tyrannical condition of some black male-female relations remains an important concern for the reality of black freedom for black female writers. Freedom is not only an external condition of society and its institutions but is equally concerned with the soul, heart, and spirit and with the desire of black people to live wholly, humanely, and optimally amid conditions of oppression and dehumanization. Such oppression and tyrannies range from the racism and discrimination of whites to those cruelties and brutalities demonstrated in the course of daily life by blacks on blacks. However the tyrannies and inhumanities manifest themselves, the quest is to break free from their diabolical hold and to realize human wholeness. This is true for black men as well as for black women.

A great gift of African American literature has been the preservation of this creative soul force and the celebration of freedom in various forms of literature. Brer Rabbit, through his crafty maneuverings and gambits, is not simply seeking personal freedom but is already demonstrating such freedom through his mother-wit and his capacity to outfox and outsmart has adversaries. That black people have been able to translate their rich oral culture to written prose is an important expression of freedom. Notwithstanding the preeminence of black oral culture, black writers, poets, and playwrights have created a literary culture that articulates the highest hopes and aspirations of African American people. It is here that the best of Euro-American culture with its emphasis on the written word has been combined with the power of the unbridled African spirit, which has given both dynamic and form to African American literature. Freedom is therefore expressed thematically as well as in the creation and use of literature as a prominent mode of communication within an oral culture.

While much of black protest literature ostensibly addresses issues around social and political freedom, a more consistent theme in African American literature has been the freedom of black people to simply be, to have, and to act in a world that has largely attempted to sequester and stifle their humanity. We see this freedom personified in Richard Wright's character, Bigger Thomas; James Baldwin, John Grimes; Langston Hughes, Simple; Ralph Ellison's nameless protagonist in *The Invisible Man*; and Toni Morrison, Pilate. While the issue of social freedom is important, ontological and spiritual freedom are equally significant.[38]

We might affirm that the recognition, preservation, celebration, and liberation of the black soul in America is a salient theme in African American literature. The Kulturkampf of the struggle for black humanity has to do with the human soul, the ability of the spirit to cry out, break free, and establish itself in a world that largely is oblivious to it and therefore devalues it as persona non grata.

The theme of black souls breaking free in literature has important implications for black life in general, for the central task of African Americans has been to realize themselves in new idioms, possibilities, and genres that establish a new and unique living hermeneutic for the black experience. An important dimension of black spirituality as a model of human freedom has been to compel black people to envision and establish their place in America through new thoughts and thoroughfares, to use culture as a means of establishing identity and a means of empowerment.

That a predominantly oral culture can appropriate the various aspects of a literary culture and use its structures as means of furthering its own objectives is a great strength of African American people. This capacity to adopt and adapt, to inform and transform the various aspects of black life through diverse idioms is a hallmark of African American freedom. This spiritual, cultural, and cognitive dexterity, which enables black people to be fluid as well as fluent, can be largely ascribed to African American spirituality. Whether it is thinking and acting in jazz configurations or developing literary excursions into the creative imagination of black poets and writers, the need invariably is to establish, celebrate, and authenticate black life as vital, wholesome, and free. This is the great statement of all black art and culture, the propensity of black souls not only to tell it like it is but also to create their own unique paradigms and constellations of thought, action, and belief that both insulate and empower black people to face, confront, embrace, surmount, and ultimately transform and liberate their human condition.

The power of black literature is not only the capacity to conceptualize matters of time, matter, and space in prose configurations, thereby establishing a new black hermeneutic among the black masses, but in the creation of a culture and spirituality wherein freedom is actualized in each creative act of the literary self that establishes and authenticates itself as an entity of superlative worth and value in relation to other selves and in a society that has historically denied its opportunities and capacity to be, think, and act literarily.

The power of white oppression for black Americans has historically resided in the capacity of white people to deny the proclivity of black people to be literary, to think, act, conceptualize, and realize themselves in terms of prose realities. The great cudgel of oppression for African Americans has not been so much the overseer's lash as it has been the systemic and insidious attempt to negate black people's propensity to establish a hermeneutic of existence that appropriates and masters the literary configurations of Anglo-American culture.

Each stroke of the black writer's pen, then, is an act of freedom, the manifestation of a discipline and freedom to develop structures that cognitively establish African Americans as codeterminers of reality. Perhaps more than any other idiom, black literature has refuted and repudiated the mythologies of black inferiority and white supremacy. That black people have the discipline, tenacity, and mind to think, act, write, and cognitively master the literary culture of their oppressors has been a freedom invariably overlooked.

By mastering the written word and literary culture, black people have destroyed the myths of black mental inferiority. Black literature has been an instrument of cultural liberation for black people not simply because of its protest content but because in the act of creating, constructing, and writing the king's English, they have affirmed themselves as cognitive equals, thus smashing the various mythologies of black nonintelligence and inferiority.

To some this might sound strange, but nowhere are the myths of white superiority affirmed and propagated more than in the areas of literature and science. It is axiomatic that because blacks are predominantly oral and rhythmic, they have trouble mastering the genres of literature and writing in literary culture, and because they cannot fathom those deeper abstract cognitive configurations, they have trouble dealing with math and science.

The point here is that black ascendancy in white literary culture has been a force for human freedom. Soul force, which is the creative fount of black creativity, is preserved and expressed in black literature as well as the extant truths of black cognitive capacities. If one can put it down on paper, express it with power, and soul, and verve, one has obtained the keys to one's own liberation and freedom.

Although the earliest slave communities were predominantly oral in communication, one cannot forget the role of two of the most important literary documents for African American life and culture: the Bible and the United States Constitution, of which we spoke earlier. In whatever forms the oral culture of African Americans manifested itself and however long blacks were not permitted to be literate, the Bible and the Constitution have always been the primary foundations to black freedom.

In other words, in an oral black culture, two important written documents had significant impact on black understandings of freedom. Although many slave preachers could not read the Bible in exhorting members of their churches, it was imaginatively and creatively used as a symbol and implement of freedom. Freedom was thus actualized in the preacher's creative use of scripture, notwithstanding his illiteracy, and in the use of the Bible as a symbol of freedom for black people both within and from the larger culture. Mastering the Bible literally meant for many the mastery of oppression and white literary culture.

We cannot exhaust all the significant dimensions of black literature as a force for liberation and transformation among black people. Suffice it to say that imaginatively, literally, or symbolically, black spirituality played an important role in keeping in the minds of black people the imperatives for surmounting their condition through a literary existence. Whether the symbolic use of scripture by preachers in those early hush harbor and plantation worship services or in the imagination dramatization of the events of scripture, the need for being literary has been an important aspect of black freedom in America. By mastering and disseminating literature, one is invariably establishing the keys to overcoming one's own oppression and domination.

Black Humor

Nothing surpasses the ability of black people to laugh heartily and viscerally. Telling a joke, signifying, being rowdy, playing the dozens, and other forms of black humor are hallmarks of African American culture. After years of pain, suffering, torture, and torment, that black Americans can still manage a smile, tell a joke, and laugh happily, is a testament to the redemptive power of God and the resiliency of the human spirit. Black humor expresses the capacity of African Americans to joyfully transform negatives into positives and to not be overwhelmed by the absurdities or futility of their plight. Humor is a celebration of the black experience. It personifies the ability of the soul to transcend and transform the tragedies of life into joyful ecstasies.

Go to any African American community and there you will find the reality of black humor. Whether it is black brothers gathering to "tell lies and signify" or churchgoers amusing themselves with the antics of church folks, the presence and power of humor is a liberating force in the lives of African Americans.

Even the horrors and terrors of slavery did not prevent African Americans from signifying on their masters and humorously mocking the hypocrisies and peccadilloes of white people in general. One slave talked of another who had the gift of humor. Sometimes they would laugh so

hard they would fall in the fields in uncontrollable fits of joy and jubilation. Not only what is said will make one laugh but how it is said. The
rhythms, inflections, and colors of black language all make the gift of
black humor even more mesmerizing. The beauty of black humor is both
the ability to laugh in the midst of pain, trouble, and sorrow and to laugh
at oneself. While African American spirituality is usually a very serious
matter, African American culture teaches the importance of enjoying life,
telling a joke, and laughing away problems and trials.

There is black humor in black communities, on the streets, in the pool
halls, barber and beauty shops, restaurants and churches, in every facet
and forum of black life in America. In taking the pulse of black America,
one invariably discovers the unmistakable presence of black laughter, humor, and jubilation. Black humor and laughter are forms of freedom for
African American people. It is practicing spiritual transcendence through
pragmatic means. To laugh at oneself and others is to not give another the
keys to personal vitality and well-being. As long as black people can
laugh at themselves and their adversaries, they will retain a freedom and
ebullience of the soul that can never be defeated by sorrow and despair.
Oppression of black people can never be consummated because although
black folks take white folks seriously, they are not taken so seriously that
they cannot be viewed humorously.

Laughter and humor have been an antidote to the noxious and depressing realities of black life in America. Laughter and humor mean freedom, power, and the capacity to transcend the boundaries, constraints,
situations, and conditions that steal black people's joy and zest for living.
African American spirituality teaches the value and power of spiritual
transcendance, rising above the debilitations and dehumanizations of
black life in America through creative and innovative means, even if it
means laughing at themselves and others to anesthetize the absurdities
and pain of black existence.

Black Art

Other important cultural forms of freedom are expressed through
painting and sculpture. In both idioms African Americans discover the
themes of freedom and vitality. The artist demonstrates the creative capacity through the creation of the art itself and dramatizes black aspirations for freedom, wholeness, and personal fulfillment. In black art, one
discovers the presence of form, content, and soul. The works of Henry Os-
sawa Tanner, Carl Owens, Aaron Douglas, Robert S. Duncanson, Fred
Jones, Romare Bearden, and others reveal the pathos and passion, fire and
fervor of black life in America.

In the creation of art, the artist not only demonstrates an intelligence, a capacity to intuit and discern the broader and more intimate dimensions of human existence, but thematically and artistically dramatizes in form, content, color, and variation the free soul and spirit that informs and influences the formation of the art itself. The spirit of soul and the creativity and mind of God are often consciously or inadvertently revealed in the works of black artists.

Multitudes of black artists both known and unknown are dedicated to the craft of painting and have produced magnificent works. The freedom and pathos, joy and pain spawning their art invariably arise from their relentless quest of the soul's search for freedom. Such soul compels African Americans to remove the barriers and shackles that sequester and impede the human spirit.

As the black artist pours his or her soul out on canvas, the human spirit soars in acts of creativity. The artist's vision is fostered by the reality of soul, which again enables him to translate to canvass what his or her soul and mind intuit and perceive through acts of spiritual transcendence. We must keep in mind that in the creation of any black works of art that symbolize and embody the spirit of black freedom, it is pure soul force that sparks its creative formation. While black artists do not always explicitly identify soul force as a foundation of their work, it is in the creation of black art that transcendence and freedom of mind and soul reach their pinnacle.

We have stated that soul force is a vital reality in African American spirituality. It is that reality which moves black people to tears or to mount up as eagles and exceed the limitations of their circumstances. This element is a differentiating and unifying force for black life as well as black art that cannot be negated.

Sports

Many of the stereotypes of black men as super-masculine menials or supermen is promulgated through sports. Black athletes are expected to perform in a superlative manner because of animal instinct and a bestial vitality. While it is true that black athletes, both male and female, have excelled in most sports in America and have distinguished themselves through their sterling performances, sports on a deeper level are a metaphor for life. That Edwin Moses and Carl Lewis have run their races with unsurpassed magnificence and dexterity and that Michael Jordan can suspend himself in midair like an eagle in flight are more than a testament to their physical conditioning as black men. It is also a metaphor for black life in general.

Michael Jordan soaring is Charlie Parker, Lewis Latimer, Ernest Everett Just, and Joseph Roberts, Jr., soaring. Carl Lewis, Jackie Joyner-Kersee, Michael Johnson, and Edwin Moses running are black people running the race of life. Muhammad Ali, Mike Tyson, and Pernell Whitaker knocking out their opponents are black people winning out over the adversaries of racism, oppression, and human devaluation. That is why when Joe Louis was knocked out by Max Schmeling, black people mourned his loss throughout the land. When Joe Louis knocked out Max Schmeling, black people, too, victoriously celebrated as if they, through Louis's prowess, triumphed over white racism and white supremacy. The symbol of defiance of authority embodied by Muhammad Ali's conscientious objection to the Vietnam War was a metaphor for black people standing up to their oppressors and actualizing self-determination. Despite criticism of his actions by many, he remained the people's champion.

The strange and mind-boggling feats that black people do with their bodies in sports is also in a strange way oppositional expression to a culture and society that has beaten that body down, roughed that body up, and ultimately castrated, lynched, and burned that body. For the black athletes to do what they please with their bodies is an antithesis, an act of freedom in relation to what white people have done to keep those bodies in check. The problem of excessive celebration demonstrated by black football players is the problem of white people atempting to check the freedom impulse of black athletes.

Creativity, transcendence, and freedom are acted out by black athletes in America. Whether it is Deion Sanders doing a dance in the end zone after scoring a touchdown or Muhammad Ali bowing in his corner on one knee giving praise and honor to Allah for the victory, the metaphor of freedom, thankfulness to God, and undaunted hope are actualized by black athletes on the playing fields and boxing rings of American sports. Black athletes provide spiritual commentary and metaphors for black life in America, and once again black spiritual belief and practice permeates its ranks.

Sports is not simply a secular excursion for black athletes but the soul's testimony to what it can do through black bodies in motion. Michael Jordan slam dunking is more than a physical event; it is a sermon, an exegesis on the soul's capacity to transcend the mundane and the profane. Wilma Rudolph's overcoming polio and winning an Olympic gold medal is a testament to the goodness and glory of God. The feats of skill, stamina, strength, and intelligence by black athletes are really acts of worship in African American culture. Sports is not simply for sports' sake but is the body's and soul's walk with God in the African American experience. Putting points on the scoreboard are oblations to the magnificent power of God in African American life. The role of African American spirituality again has had significant impact in shaping the spiritual metaphors of black sports for black life in America.

Dance and the Choreography of Black Freedom

Dance is an important form of worship in the African American experience. The spiritual implications of this art form are very important for African American people. It suggests the power to move black bodies gracefully, defiantly, forcefully, and artistically through time and space. Dance has always been a significant part of African and African American culture. Dance means the capacity to choreograph certain movements for artistic and spiritual purposes. It is reshaping black reality according to the choreography of the artist. Black dancers and their audiences experience therapy, catharsis, and transcendence. Dance is not only a creative expression that articulates the thoughts, sensations, and perceptions of the soul, but it also actualizes a more profound attempt by black artists to write their own steps, perform their own music, and create their own reality.

In a racist society where some behavior, thought, expression, and belief is zealously dictated and "choreographed" by white racists, dance personifies the attempt of black souls and bodies to rechoreograph the script of reality according to a higher spiritual purpose. Dance, in part, represents the attempt of black artists and dancers to reshape black reality according to a new choreography, one not predetermined by white or other folks, one that encapsulates the desire of black people to determine who they wholly are, express who they really are, and realize who they fully want to be.

Virtually every movement, thought, behavior, and belief of blacks have incited some racist whites into believing that they have the right to control, order, or dictate black actions according to some previously choreographed notion of white behavioral norms in order to reinforce white hegemony. One sees this in every area of black life from recommendations about what constitutes acceptable black behavior vis-à-vis white people, to taboos about black men not gazing too long at white women. White racism and oppression have been one giant attempt to choreograph and automate black behavior for white domination and subjugation. Black dance transcends all attempts by the larger culture to determine how African Americans will walk and talk, what they will think and what they will believe in determining black reality.

Black dance is the artistic expression of the black body's and soul's attempt at self-determination in order to rechoreograph black life according to black culture, spirituality, and consciousness. Whether it is dancing in the barroom, the church hall, or the amphitheater, it all simulates contact with a higher reality and creates its own litanies of release from the pain and peril of oppression and dehumanization.

Black dance is an expression of black freedom and the foundation again is African American spiritual belief. As a practice of creativity and physical transcendence, black dance is a liberating and transforming force in African American spirituality and culture. To dance gracefully and defiantly, to move deftly through space and time, is to discover that dimension of reality and being that transcends the dimensions of life itself. This is freedom. To express with black bodies what white bodies cannot express and to move and interpret with black bodies that have been beaten, bullied, and burdened is not only an act of humanity and artistic creativity but also the expression of freedom in African American life. That body and soul can provide some creative expression for life, however burdened and oppressed, is a gift of human freedom and a kingpin of African American spirituality.

The Science of Black Life

There is a science to black life inherent in black culture. Creigs Beverly, citing a Ghanaian proverb, epitomized it with the statement, "It is seeing the music and hearing the dance."[39] The science of black life culminates in the laws of reversed meanings and efforts, the rules of arriving at direction through indirection, and a whole matrix of thoughts, beliefs, and actions designed to bedazzle, weaken, and baffle their adversaries. This means that whatever one says about black life and culture, they can never really and forthrightly figure out black folk because there will always be coded meanings and cryptic modes of communication, configurations of behavior and belief that defy and subvert all attempts by the larger culture to discern, ultimately determine, and dominate it.

The science of black life ultimately means that black people will finally determine for themselves what is true, beautiful, and valuable and that the rights, privileges of being, acting, and thinking as persons are essentially determined by the ethos and culture, the spirituality and beliefs of African Americans themselves. Miles Davis expressed it beautifully when a white critic asked the key to his music. "I play what's not there on the paper."

The science of African American life is rooted in the idea that all ultimate verifications of what is real, bona fide, and true for black people must be determined by black people and that any realization of authentic existence must have as its foundation black culture and spirituality.

What's up is down.
What's down is up.
What you think you know
you don't know
and what you don't know
you do know.

Some writers have observed that a culture of deception has been developed by black people in order to survive in America. James Cone and Howard Thurman delineate the reality of deception on the plantation and discuss how slaves employed it as a way of manipulating their masters.[40] If deception meant staying alive and establishing the moral high ground, it was thoroughly used. The problem here as Thurman has observed is that the one who deceives becomes a deception. Moral authority is abdicated because of fear and failure to use truth as soul force for liberation.

The science of black life suggests that the nature, style, culture, ethos, ethics, values, and concerns of black people are filtered through the cultural and spiritual prisms of African Americans. This means that oppressors and adversaries of African American people shall never possess the key to black determination because the spirituality, culture, and science of black existence have instilled within African Americans a resiliency and resolve to live life on their own terms. There will always be what Bob Marley called a natural mystic blowing through the air of black life, a reality that cannot be fully fathomed or determined by other people, one that will maintain its own integrity, dignity, and hegemony in spite of efforts to delegitimize, devalue, and ultimately negate or destroy it.

Because the ultimate autonomous, hegemonic reality in African American spirituality is God, black people have continued to express and live freely. One can never be fully oppressed as long as one uses culture and spirituality as a means of shaping, valuing, transcending, and transforming reality. This is the science of black existence: to live forthrightly, innovatively, and improvisationally so that no people, even though they kill the body, will ultimately determine the sanctity, value, and worth of black life. African Americans have always used their culture and spirituality as a force for human freedom, and the use of these two entities distinguishes the African American paradigm from other models of freedom.

The Blessed Power
of Black Culture

We cannot exhaust all aspects of African American culture. Suffice it to say that black culture in America has nurtured the reality of soul force as a creative fount to the creation of black consciousness, spirituality, and culture. While black people historically because of slavery, white racism, and oppression have not been physically, socially, or politically free in the sense that white Americans have been, they have nonetheless created a spirituality of culture and a culture of spirituality that has enabled them to create, define, and determine reality and their place in it on their own terms. While political, social, and relational freedom may have been a will-o'-the-wisp for African Americans, they have used culture and spirituality as a means of defying the culture of their adversaries while carving out an ethos of existence that has reinforced their sanity, survival, and vitality.

From the earliest days of black life in America, the practice of black belief and spirituality has created an ethos or sanctuary in which African Americans could soulfully express and define themselves and create a reality that preserved and reinforced their unique identity as a people. In the early hush arbor and camp meetings black people practiced spirituality as a vehicle for creating a culture of opposition, affirmation, and creativity in relation to the status quo. In other words, as black people came together to pray, preach, praise, dance, sing, and shout, they created the context for the formation of a spirituality of culture and a culture of spirituality that would empower them to interpret, shape, and ultimately transform reality on their own terms. If blacks were not socially free because of white racism, they could fashion a cultural and spiritual ethos that expressed, preserved, and ultimately transformed their existential condition through soul force.

Thus the creation of a revolution in music through jazz was certainly as important to black freedom, sanity, and vitality as a political revolution that was virtually impossible. Musician Archie Shepp expressed it with these words:

> The Negro musician is a reflection of the Negro people as a social phenomenon. His purpose ought to be to liberate America aesthetically and socially from its inhumanity. The inhumanity of the white American to the black American, as well as the inhumanity of the white American to the white American, is not basic to America and can be exorcised.[41]

Malcolm X drew a correlation between black political and cultural freedom in citing the improvisation of the black jazz musician:

> The white musician can jam if he's got some sheet music in front of him. He can jam on something that he's heard jammed before. But that black musician, he picks up his horn and starts blowing

some sounds that he never thought of before. He improvises, he creates, it comes from within. It's his soul; it's that soul music. It's the only area on the American scene where the black man has been free to create. And he has mastered it. He has shown that he can come up with something that nobody ever thought of on his own. . . . He will improvise; he'll bring it from within himself. And this is what you and I want.[42]

The point here is that soul culture and spirituality have functioned as propellants for freedom among African Americans. Cultural and spiritual freedom emerges from black soul force and creativity. Being free from a black perspective means freedom to create soul culture and spirituality that reinforce sanity, serenity, and spiritual vitality.

At issue here is the freedom to create, define, and express reality through one's own values and eyes, and this is a definitive hallmark of African American freedom. Freedom is not simply the ability to move about geographically, interact with white people as equals, or run for political office. It is freedom to create internally, cognitive and emotive structures, a hermeneutic or prism of the world that ensures black dignity, creative power, and survival. Such internal freedom, the capacity to create culture, is possible through the practice of soul force spirituality. Black spirituality has always emphasized the importance of preserving soul freedom, freedom to respond to and define reality on black terms rather than white terms. This is the great gift of African American spirituality and culture.

Whether it is creating or singing the blues, spirituals, gospel, jazz, or the classics, it all stems from the freedom and power of the human spirit to name, define, determine, and express itself according to the trajectories and entreaties of God and the human spirit. It is here that dignity is preserved and an autonomy of the head, heart, and soul are actualized.

As long as black people can create culture through soul force, they possess the freedom to determine the ultimate ground of their human existence. Black culture and black spirituality have been forces for amalgamation, transformation, and liberation of African American people in Anglo-American society. Any serious study of the history of freedom must consider the paradigm African Americans have created through the practice of culture and spirituality. To name, define, express, embrace, create, transform, and transcend the culture and oppressive realities of white culture and society have been important dimensions of African American freedom.

The results of such praxis is black people's capacity to choose a course of existence that preserves soul force and spirit, actualizes humanity, and empowers the fulfillment of human possibilities and potential. That black people have been able to accomplish this in such large measure is greatly ascribed to the practice of black culture and spirituality as a humanizing, radicalizing, and liberating force for African American people.

The development of black culture and spirituality has enabled black people to oppose, defy, and ultimately transcend those debilitating realities of culture and society that reduce, devalue, delegitimize, and attempt to destroy African American's sense of personal value and worth. That black people have come this far with some semblance of vitality and pride is largely due to the fact that black culture and spirituality created an ethos in which they could express themselves, oppose an evil system, and survive the holocaust of black dehumanization.

Six

Spirituality and Freedom in Worship

Black worship is the experience where the ritual dramas of freedom are actualized in the African American church. Black worship is more than praising and celebrating God and "how I got over." It is the theater or forum wherein the dreams, ritual dramas, aspirations, and affirmation of freedom for black souls and spirits are actualized in a corporate context. Black worship is the arena in which creative soul force is nurtured, reified, and reaffirmed and the ethos where black culture and spirituality are created, interpreted, and expressed.

We have stated throughout this book that the uniqueness of the African American paradigm of human freedom lies precisely in the way black Americans have used culture and spirituality as creative soul force in naming, defining, creating, and transforming black existence. It has been through the creation of these interior modalities of being, culture, spirituality, and existence that African Americans have developed a paradigm of spiritual and cultural freedom that has facilitated their survival as an oppressed people. The use of culture as a force for liberation was initially fostered under the aegis of spiritual praxis when blacks gathered at hush arbors and camp meetings to tell the story, depict their condition, and dramatize their quest for human freedom. It was in these early and nightly convenings that an ethos or culture of freedom was formed where blacks could create a spiritual and cultural reality that would affirm their value, worth, and identity as human persons.

Thus the spirituals are the result of this cultural and spiritual freedom made possible through the unbridled actualization of creative soul force. The celebration of God and the redemptive power of God's Spirit created a context in which blacks could freely explore, express, construct, and transform their existential condition. If blacks were not socially free to be full citizens in society, they were culturally and spiritually free to construct their own reality, insulate themselves from the terrors of dehumanization and subjugation, and still manage to live with dignity by choosing humane modes of response to their debilitating and often depressing conditions.

The African American paradigm of freedom is realized in the way blacks have used culture and spirituality through creative soul force in facing, embracing, transcending, and transforming the constraints and perils of their human condition. It has also allowed them to adopt and adapt the culture of their captors and translate it into meaningful liturgies of survival. Thus each act of black worship is both a celebration of the spirit of freedom through the praxis of culture and spirituality and a creation of a culture that sustains black vitality and freedom. In worship God is affirmed and the promise and potentiality of black life sustained.

Symbiosis is an important concept here because black worshipers experience the full contiguity of living with God and in community with others. More than any other spiritual experience, black worship dramatizes the rituals of black life and corporately connects black worshipers with divine reality through multiple idioms of empowerment. Worship has historically been the place where black souls could freely express themselves, interpret, and transform reality through divine invocation and intervention and ultimately transcend the devastations of their existential condition.

Moreover, worship is a vehicle of cultural and spiritual freedom and has helped establish the uniqueness of the African American paradigm of freedom. Placing the value of black Christian worship in historical perspective, Melva Wilson Costen makes the following observation about the meaning of worship for black slaves:

> Separate and apart from those who denied them freedom on earth, slaves were free in worship to hear and respond to the Word of God. They could hear and recall the message of salvation and deliverance and increase their faith in God, whose Son, Jesus, had overcome earthly suffering. They could find mental and emotional release in spite of their physical enslavement. They could experience the freedom of verbal and nonverbal expression. They could give and receive affirmation, support, and encouragement. They could worship God with their whole being. They dared to risk the punishment they would surely receive if their Invisible Institution became visible to the slave masters.[1]

Celebration

Worship is the celebration of God and life and the Spirits' power to overcome evil, heal lives, and bring about personal and collective transformation. To celebrate corporately the reality of God under conditions of oppression and domination is a triumph of human freedom. "How shall we sing the LORD's song in a foreign land?" (Ps. 137:4, RSV). The celebrative worship style of many African Americans is at once a corporate recognition of the goodness, power, and glory of God and an affirmation of how far God has brought them. Celebrating the spirit of God and life itself is an expression of human freedom. To celebrate is to break free from convention and constraint, proscription and prohibition. It is the power of creative soul force to assert and express itself as vital, life-affirming, and sustaining reality.

The spirit of celebration in black worship is an alternative expression to the more reticent and contemplative forms of worship in various Anglo churches. Black people have made a point to worship freely and enthusiastically not only because God has been good to them but also in objection to the cultural and spiritual constraints of Anglo-American culture.

Black worship is at times a cultural subversion of polite, genteel white cultural values. Black worship fervently values, corroborates, and celebrates black life. It is the objective of black souls to celebrate life, God, and "how I got over" in a world that frenetically tries to destroy and stymie it. Each expression of celebration in worship is not only adulation of God but the affirmation of the power of black soul force as an instrument of black freedom. The black soul must find spiritual and cultural expression. This is the essence of the African American freedom. It therefore must assert itself, realize itself, even rediscover and transform itself in the context of the worship experience.

It is here that the glorious, redemptive, apocalyptic, and miraculous intervention of God and the Holy Spirit blaze their trails of spiritual transformation in the minds, hearts, and souls of black believers. The celebrative dimensions of black culture and spirituality reach their apex in African American Christian worship. It is through an invocation of the Holy Spirit, evocation of those cultural idioms and vehicles that facilitate free soul expression that lead to the demonstration of freedom in black worship. Every act of worship in this regard is consciously or unconsciously an expression and manifestation of human freedom.

Affirmation

To celebrate in worship is finally to declare that God is still in charge of all our affairs, and despite what has happened to black people, it is not as important as what happens in them through spiritual transformation. Worship, therefore, is an affirmation of life and the power of God to sustain and translate that life into meaningful expressions of vitality. Such affirmation is also a ceremonial and ritual acknowledgment that God is the supreme source of life and that a genuine relationship with God is the élan vital of black existence.

We wrote earlier of the corroborative function of African American spirituality where values are created and clarified for the legitimation and empowerment of black life. By affirming the redemptive, liberating, and sanctifying grace and power of God in black life, African Americans are valuing the role of spirituality in shaping consciousness, belief, and behavior among African Americans. Worship is the place such values are actualized as believers ritually and ceremonially connect with divine reality. To worship in the black experience is to affirm all that God has done, can do, and will do amid existential circumstances. Worship thus has a sacralizing function in the African American experience, for it provides believers with opportunities to corporately acknowledge the sacredness of black existence.

Translation

A central focus of black spirituality is to enable black people to translate the absurdities and atrocities of their experience into meaningful idioms of vitality and reality. A primary goal of black freedom in the praxis of black spirituality is to equip African Americans with the spiritual and practical resources that help them surmount the limitations of their human condition.

Worship is the ritual dramatization of the power and Spirit of God to translate lives into conscious awareness of their own powers and properties, their own gifts and graces. When divine intervention and consciousness coalesce, new translations of human life are made possible. As a vehicle of freedom, black worship thus enables African Americans to freely shape, sculpt, and translate into new realities of hope, faith, love, truth, and power, the realities of black pain, suffering, dehumanization, discrimination, and domination. The language, litanies, and liturgies of black worship as expressed through music, preaching, healing, and praying all have profound influences in the translation process.

When the world told black people they were less than human, worship empowered them to translate themselves into a new identity as children of God. When denied and despised by the larger culture because of their black skin, African Americans found that worship provided a creative and cultural ethos where such aspersions could be altered into life-sustaining possibilities. The liberating power of black worship lies in its ability to translate black life into meaningful texts of praise, spirituality, and human empowerment.

Transformation

Another important dimension of black worship is the consecration that is actualized through the ritual dramas and ceremonies of African American spiritual worship. Each act of worship is inherently an act of consecration, of connecting with divine reality for the purposes of interpretation and empowerment. To make holy, clean, and righteous amid the diabolical forces of life is a significant aspect of black worship. Among the many sacred and liturgical functions of black worship, none is more eminent than its power to transform black life into a positive experience. Worship, for our purposes, is the ultimate corporate act of human transformation in relation to divine reality. The great expectations of black worship lie precisely in the assumption that God will change things for the better and that God did not bring anyone this far to leave them.

The preaching, teaching, praising, singing, healing, and delivering of black worship is a ceremonial and ritual acknowledgment of how God has changed and will change things for the better. Thus in worship the expectation of spiritual liberation is actualized in the reality of spirits and bodies breaking free in joyful and festive transformation, in the enthusiastic singing and preaching of the Word, and in the power of imagination, ritual, and the hermeneutics of survival to intersect into meaningful litanies of spiritual, social, and relational empowerment among black people. A primary theme of black Christian worship is that change will come through the Spirit's invocation. In the evocation of creative soul force, black lives will realize human potential, healing, and wholeness.

Worship is the centering and unifying fount of black spiritual consciousness. It is here that the hopeful and confident expectations of God's liberating possibilities are transformed into creative and expressive modalities of hope, vitality, and renewal. Nicholas Cooper Lewter and Henry Mitchell describe these as core beliefs of the black experience.[2]

Melva Wilson Costen is again helpful by delineating how worship as an expression of core beliefs affirms for the black community other important elements that in my estimation are essential to human freedom:

> A persistent negative attitude toward African primal religions has made it difficult to acknowledge the inheritance of primal worldviews and core beliefs. Nevertheless, there are sufficient data to substantiate the "primal" acceptance of the unity and wholeness of life, which is evident in African American communal life, religion and worship, music, art, politics, and culture. The outward expressions of feelings and emotions, the tendency to "move with the beat," the similarity of music for worship and music for entertainment all speak to the functioning of an

underlying belief system. A system of beliefs imposed by the dominant culture could not and cannot be a viable belief system for a marginalized people. A belief system, already well established in African traditions, continues to help an oppressed community find meaning and make sense of life, maintain community identity and continuity, find direction, and provide healing and empowerment.[3]

Regarding the symbols of worship, Costen is also extremely helpful:

> African peoples respond to God's presence in a variety of ways. Responses may be formal or informal, spontaneous or regularized, personal or communal. Worship is generally expressed vocally and physically rather than meditationally. Beliefs as well as ritual actions are related to the lived experiences of the community. . . . Through symbols the community expresses what might be difficult to verbalize. Symbols help "free" the mind of clutter so that clarity can be given to phenomena that might otherwise be incomprehensible. Music, movement, physical gestures, colors, shapes, and the gifts of nature common to the community are very important symbols.[4]

The power of transformation is realized by the use of symbols, moving with the rhythm of the Spirit, and being transported into other realms of the spiritual cosmos. Every aspect of black worship is rife with the possibility of human transformation, a great hallmark of African American spiritual freedom. The signs, symbols, ritual dramas, and the forms and content of the ceremonies and liturgies of black worship create their own archive of black cultural and spiritual survival. Accordingly, many blacks have not only viewed the worship experience as a reenactment and actualization of God's transformative powers but have subconsciously appropriated the forms and dynamics of black worship as vehicles for creating and transforming culture and other areas of black existence.

It is less important to be transformed in worship than it is to transform existing realities through those modalities and liturgies of worship that sacralize life. That is to say, the worship that empowers black souls to freely and creatively express themselves in transformative acts of praise, prayer, healing, singing, and sermonizing are manifested in other aspects of black life and culture. For example, letting the spirit freely soar is not only found in worship but also expressed in creating and sustaining black culture, thus profoundly influencing other dimensions of the black experience. Freedom of the spirit is thus actualized as freedom of the mind, body, and soul to dramatize and express its core beliefs and ultimate concerns.

Because God transforms life in myriad ways, worship becomes a vehicle for the acknowledgment and establishment of those transformative modalities that empower and vitalize black existence. It is not enough to experience spiritual transformation. Acting as agencies of freedom and worship, the individual must also transform existing reality into some meaningful litanies of empowerment. One goes to church to experience spiritual transformation in worship. Thus each subsequent act of worship in daily experience is a testament to the Spirit's power to transform all reality, socially, politically, economically, and relationally.

The following forms of worship are also expressions of freedom for African American people. Their symbols, signs, actions, and ritual dramas all represent a larger reality of human freedom for black people in America.

Forms of Worship

Prayer

Prayer is a vehicle of human freedom because it connects the believer with a higher cosmic reality. The power of prayer lies not only on its transformative possibilities but also in the invocation of a larger consciousness and power that mediate through human experience. Minister Fred Sampson, at Tabernacle Baptist Church in Detroit, Michigan, has often said, "Don't just say a prayer, but be a prayer." Here prayer is not simply a ritual or ceremonial act that the individual engages in to solicit divine intervention, but it becomes a vehicle that translates and transforms the believer according to its own purposes. The purpose of prayer is thus not only to pray but also to be used and transformed by divine reality according to some higher purpose.

Black prayer has always been a form of freedom not simply because it connects believers with divine reality but also because it shapes consciousness, culture, spirituality, and core beliefs. The rhythm and power of prayer creates its own litanies and liturgies of human dignity and survival. It infuses human consciousness with an awareness of divine reality. Divine reality cannot be experienced and affirmed without the self undergoing transformation. Every act of prayer that presupposes a revelation of God results in the transformation of the believer's consciousness of time, space, and reality. When perceptions of time, space, and reality are altered, the possibilities of both self and God are reconfigured. Black prayer thus has medicinal and transformative value because it is a vehicle for the intersection and transformation of human and divine consciousness.

Black prayer has been a vital force of liberation for African American people because it allows free expression of the mind, soul, and heart and is part of the spiritual empowerment process of African American peoples. In black prayer there is a rhythm and power that flows with the rhythms of the cosmos. The rhythmic cadences of black prayer create their own power and awareness of God's presence. Listen to black people praying and at once discover a poetry of the soul laid bare, a melodic turning and phraseology that is both medicinal and therapeutic. This rhythm is found in the ebb and flow of the sea, in the crest and fall of stars in orbit, in the hum, moan, and elongated groan of blues, gospel and jazz singers, in the amen corners and hallelujah choruses of black churches, in the call and response, style and profile of black life and culture. Prayer is the power cord of black salvation and liberation, the umbilical cord of the black lifeline to God.

Where would black people be without prayer? Without prayer they would have perished in despair long ago. In the darkened, vermin-infested holes of slaver's ships, prayers bound black souls across tribal lines and gave them a common ground for hope. On plantations beyond the gazing eyes of masters and overseers, prayers energized, sustained, and even transported slaves into other realms. Prayer is a unifying force, a bulwark against evil, and a means of spiritual transportation and imagination. Today in African American communities prayer is the guiding light of black lives.

So long as black people can pray, there is always recourse to meliorate their human condition because God is ultimately in charge and will have the final say in all matters. John S. Mbiti delineates the scope of African prayers, which is certainly the foundation of African American prayer traditions:

> In the prayers man addresses God as his Father, Creator, Protector, Provident. Man acknowledges spiritual realities of which God is supreme. Man speaks to these realities, addressing nine-tenths of his prayers to God and one-tenth to the other invisible realities. Thus, man is concerned with both his physical and spiritual welfare. He wants to be in harmony with the world in which he is living.[5]

Aylward Shorter says it is the central phenomenon in African religion, often indistinguishable from verbal magic. Prayer provides a form of control over one's environment.[6] Controlling the terrors and uncertainties of the environment has made prayer a vital force in the lives of African Americans. The prayer traditions of black Americans are cultivated in every area of black life, but the church remains the unsurpassed spiritual station where prayer is celebrated and acknowledged as the dominant spiritual source of black life in America.

Because black soul force is such an important factor in creating and sustaining those elements of culture and spirituality that engender black freedom, prayer is a significant source of nurturing. Without prayer the creative soul force of black people could not imagine, create, sustain, energize, embrace, and ultimately transform African American existence. Prayer is the oasis of black soul force.

Each opportunity to pray in church and in other areas of black life is not only an expression of soul force but a means of enabling that force to set the course of life through personal expression. The black church is the place where the actualization of soul force through prayer becomes a unifying and transforming power for human freedom. When black people come together to share, celebrate, and pray this soul force into reality, it is an affirmation of the inherent spiritual power of black people to transform existing conditions.

In other words, black people have always believed there is power in prayer. Sometimes when the saints are praying, one can see the immediate transformation or transfiguration of the individual. Perhaps a disease is miraculously healed or someone is converted to Christ. Whatever the case, the physical manifestation of prayer's power is often demonstrated in the worship services of African Americans. These experiences of transformation and healing in the corporate context have done more to bolster black empowerment and freedom than some political forms of agitation. The major place where black people actualize their spiritual and creative powers of transformation is in the worship service of the black church, where lives are healed, transformed, and delivered through the power of prayer. This has made more of a statement about black freedom and power than some political forms of freedom expressed in the social arena. Moreover, we might even affirm that the success of those political, social, cultural, and other forms of freedom for African Americans is precisely because of the transforming power of prayer. That black people can evidence the results of prayer right before their very eyes in worship reinforces black spiritual power and freedom in the minds of African American people.

Prayer also has liturgical, sacralizing, and social functions. It allows black people to invoke divine presence and allow themselves to be used as instruments of healing, liberation, and transformation. The transcendent awareness of such profound spiritual power does much to sacralize black life as something worthy and holy in God's sight. The fact that black people can heal, transform, and deliver through the power of prayer and spirituality means that God is working in and through them despite what has happened to them in the larger society. Those who have been profaned and desecrated are now worthwhile and holy in the eyes of God. Those who have been cast aside and repudiated are now used as instruments of redemption and spiritual transformation. As long as black people can find the power, faith, and courage to pray, they can express themselves as free persons in an oppressive society. Prayer helps them maintain a vital and living relationship with God. Without God, African Americans would have perished in the doldrums of depression and despair in America.

Healing

Healing is an important part of the African American spiritual tradition. The need for healing and wholeness has always been a central element in African American life. The church is the healing center and worship is the healing balm for black lives. A saving grace of the black church is that it has always recognized itself as a place of refuge and healing for the lost, lonely, broken, the depressed, and oppressed. Spiritual, physical, psychological, and relational healing have been realized in the lives of black believers.

Worship provides healing as the community of faith comes together collectively to affirm their ultimate concerns. It is realized through ritual ceremonies and liturgies of the church, through the testimonies and power of God's work in their lives. The fellowship of black churches through their extended families and networks of personal, vocational, and familial affirmation also make the black church a place of healing. Healing comes in response to the troubles and sorrows of this life. It is affirmed through prayer, preaching, counseling, laying on of hands, anointing with oil, and other ritual ceremonies of the black church.

Worship becomes one of the most important instruments of healing for African Americans because it is the place of corporate acknowledgment, affirmation, and celebration of the goodness and power of God that collectively reinforces spiritual strength. Many black churches have testimonial moments in the service because they have long recognized the dynamics of group therapy, that by sharing concerns in the context of community various processes of identification and healing can take place for individuals. One of the most important aspects of any form of healing is listening. When persons can have their concerns heard by a larger body of caring believers, they can begin the healing process and find solace and comfort in being part of a larger network of spiritual believers. Worship is the forum where believers are assured that God still cares for them, loves them, and ultimately wants to heal their lives. The music, preaching, teaching, and reaching of black worship also provides healing for the broken and lost.

Healing is an expression of cultural and spiritual freedom in worship because black people are free to express themselves and invoke divine deliverance from their pain. The black church has always provided a context in which black souls could be laid bare before God and others, resulting in wholeness and well-being. Freedom is not only actualized in the black church through various forms of healing but also in black people knowing that they have a place where they can be themselves and express the deepest longings and ultimate concerns of their souls. The praxis of freedom is thus realized in the ability of the soul to express its issues of life and death and to develop idioms of healing and caring that will restore it to wholeness.

African Americans have experienced the healing that freedom of spiritual expression affords. They know what it means to have their hearts, bodies, souls, and spirits mended through the praxis of faith in community. Knowing they have a place to go to petition the great God of healing for the troubles they have seen has had enormous impact on their overall wellness, wholeness, and spiritual vitality. They have come this far through their healing. They will continue their journey because of a healing God who cares for and loves them.

Shouting

An essential element of black freedom is that creative soul force must express itself through the creation of culture and the expression of spirituality. These are the twin engines of black humanity and vitality, and they culminate in a black ethos that values the power of personal expression. Shouting is an expression of freedom. It is the voice of the soul verbalizing itself in worship. It is release from the social and relational bondage that comes from living black in a racist society. It is the ultimate emblem of the freedom of creative soul force.

Ralph Wiley put it this way:

> Why do black people tend to shout? Now there is a question for the ages. Black people tend to shout in churches, movie theaters, and anywhere else they feel the need to shout, because when joy, pain, anger, confusion and frustration, ego and thought, mix it up, the way they do inside black people, the uproar is too big to hold inside. The feeling must be aired.
>
> Black people tend to shout because nothing has come close to making those of the African Diaspora less determined, or less artistic, or less inventive, or less adaptable, or less productive, or less wise, or less creative, or less quite stupendously gorgeous. Black people shout because they are immortal and sense this. Black people sense this because we have been dying, yet here black people are, the salt of the earth. Here we are.[7]

Shouting is not only an insignia of freedom in the black church but is manifested in every area of black life and culture: music, preaching, poetry, laughing, work, celebration, and fellowship. The shout of celebration and freedom of the soul is ever-present in black life. Musicians shout on their instruments. Preachers shout in their sermons. Audiences shout in their laughter, amens, and other responses. Rappers, signifiers, and testifiers shout in their soliloquies, and their recipients shout in reply. Writers shout in their writing! Shouting is emblematic of the freedom of black soul force and a direct antithesis to the reticence of white cultural norms and values.

To shout is to break silence, to ruffle still waters, to subvert convention, to challenge the values and assumptions of the status quo. The black shout on Sunday morning is not only an affirmation of the power of God to save and transform black lives but also a therapeutic, healing catharsis that throws off the trouble, pain, penalty, persecution, and prosecution of the larger society. Rather than visit the psychiatrist, black people shout out the things that both trouble and lift them. The shout can be praise or protest, resistance or conformation to the present reality.

For many whites and some blacks, shouting represents primitive forms of spiritual expression. It was, and still is, considered by the more educated elite to be uncouth and uncultured. To shout is to lose control, to allow the emotions to override the intellect and more genteel behavior. Despite this view, shouting has had therapeutic and medicinal value for black people over the years. Whether they are shouts of joy or shouts of pain, they ultimately signify the power of black creative soul force breaking free from the constraints, conventions, hypocrisies, and conspiracies of silence enforced by Anglo-American culture and belief. It is to defy what Albert Camus called "the unreasonable silence of the world."[8]

For black people in America a code or conspiracy of silence by whites and others enveloped their world for too long. Too many atrocities and crimes have been committed against African Americans where others have stood or sat in silence, allowing the evils to be perpetrated. The black culture soul and creative soul force have always boldly refuted the codes of silence and reticence caused by oppression and discrimination in American society. It is the nature of the black soul force to realize itself by freely, boldly, and undauntedly expressing its core beliefs and values in direct defiance to the culture of silence created by intimidation and oppression. Thus an ultimate act of freedom is to speak boldly and frankly to these concerns, culturally, spiritually, personally, and socially. It is to compel black soul force to express and actualize itself under conditions of terror and oppression.

Herbert Marcuse termed this force breaking free from the constraints of domination as "surplus repression."[9] As a result of racial repression and oppression reinforced through the culture of silence, black people found modalities of expression that appeared innocuous in their manifestation but were really personal exemplifications of freedom. Shouting is simply another aspect of this freedom of the soul to break free and express itself despite what other folks do or think. A people who have had to be so concerned about what white people thought about them and did to them, had to develop instruments of personal expression and survival that would give them some semblance of freedom and vitality. Shouting provided this vehicle for African Americans and is still used today as a form of spiritual freedom for black celebration and empowerment.

To express oneself from the core of concern, from the depths of the soul without wonder or worry about repercussions and recriminations is a hallmark of black freedom. In a society where so much is judged on how well people restrain themselves, and intelligence is associated with the absence of passion and emotion, shouting is the ultimate subversion. In a culture where intelligence, poise, culture, and power are based on how well one keeps to oneself those critical matters of ultimate and vital concern, shouting is the quintessence of spiritual and cultural insurrection. To shout is to call attention to something that people would much rather forget.

Even in some black churches, shouting is frowned upon: "We don't do that here!" The ultimate act of eccelesiastical subreption is to shout in a Sunday morning service when the decorum is quietistic. Shouting thus is part of the liturgy of black life. It is sacred expression of black souls laid bare before God. It is part of the litany of celebration and thanksgiving of "how I got over" and "how God made a way out of no way" amid the turbulence and turmoil of living black in a racist society.

Praising

Another important element of black worship is praise. Thanksgiving and praise of God for all one's many blessings is an integral element in African American worship. That black Americans can praise God after all they have gone through in America is a miracle. That black people have been blessed in America is also a great blessing.

Praise is significant because it is an affirmation of God's goodness under difficult circumstances. Although many African Americans lament having gone through the pain of racism and oppression, many of them are both thankful and grateful for coming through such experiences relatively unscathed. Furthermore, whatever is said about the evils and injustices of America, many black people are proud to be Americans. They take great pride and joy in being part of this country and readily celebrate and acknowledge God's goodness through it all. It takes a certain courage, strength, pride, and power to still hold one's head up high and praise God for the good things of this life. This has been a great strength of the African American church. Encouraging and enabling black Americans to be faithful, hopeful, and praising of God amid the errors and terrors of American life attests to the power of spirituality and creative soul force as vital elements of freedom.

Praising God is redemptive, healing, and ultimately life-affirming. Claiming spiritual victory after going through many "dangers, toils, and snares" is a strength of African American spiritual praxis and belief. Notwithstanding the trouble, sorrow, disappointment, and despair, praising God will lift burdens and chase away problems for a night.

A great gift of African American churches is their praise orientation of the gifts of life. Sorrow will never have the last word in African American churches because blacks have been taught to look up, to be thankful, and to praise God always for the blessings of life. Praise is thus part of the sacred liturgy of black life in America. It raises expectations about God's redemptive work among "the least of these " in human history and enables people to see their lives in a more joyous light. Nothing can ever be so reprehensible that the goodness of God cannot be acknowledged, affirmed, or celebrated.

This spirit of praise and celebration, nascent spiritual fruit of black soul force, this determination to affirm God "in spite of" has been one of the most important elements shaping black freedom and vitality. An optimistic and resilient self-determination remains in African Americans, instilled by spiritual belief and the church, that nothing in this life will retain the power to snuff out the praise lights of African American people. This praise of God and celebration of life and culture are the guiding forces of black existence in America. Nothing will destroy the capacity of black people to live, love, praise, and affirm the redemptive, transforming, liberating power of God. This power is manifested even in black relations with blacks, in black relations with whites and others, in every aspect of the culture, mythos, and ethos of African Americans.

If anything has been the African American's gift to America, it has been the ability to live life fully, wholly, and positively amid continual forces of dehumanization and subjugation. Living largely without malice, hatred, and evil for adversaries has been one of the great triumphs of the human spirit anywhere and at any time in human history. The spirit of praise, where life and God are exalted as glorious gifts, has been a beacon for the freedom, liberation, and well-being of African American people. This central fact is an incontrovertible truth for black people. That black people can praise joyfully is a testament to the power and goodness of God.

Again, many critics of this aspect of black life and culture have been too quick to dismiss this reality as simplistic and servile. Praising away one's problems is simply another means of avoiding responsibility for coming to terms with and resolving the critical socio-political problems facing black Americans. While this view contains elements of truth, the overriding belief is that praise for God has been a unifying and liberating element of black soul force and that the spiritual unleashing of that force has influenced the will to freedom in every area of black life.

Thus praising God in a culture and society that has done everything it could to remove such praise from the lips of black Americans is a Herculean manifestation of the freedom and power of black soul force as an instrument of human liberation. It is not a diversion from responsibility but a titan affirmation of the power of the soul to live, think, and act and the power of God to redeem, transform, and liberate those souls into meaningful reality. Too often, critics of the black church and black spirituality have failed to fathom how these entities, with the infusion of black soul force, have enabled black Americans to live with dignity, hope, strength, courage, and love in a society that largely despised, rejected, and dominated them. For any black person to have the courage to praise God under such conditions is a remarkable tour de force of the human spirit and an essential element of African American freedom. To pray and praise God in a world that assiduously tried to remove every rational human basis for the celebration of life and divine reality is a hallmark of black freedom.

To verbalize such sentiments and ideas of God demonstrates the preponderance of oral culture among black Americans. To shout, pray, and praise enthusiastically is to express a freedom of the soul that can never be discomfited or sequestered by social and political realities. This same freedom of the soul is the fuel of black culture and black spirituality and the predominant shaper of black consciousness, identity, belief, and destiny.

Dancing

To dance in worship is to put the whole body into praise activity. Emanating from Africa, black dance has always been a vital expression of black worship and part of the sacralizing activity of black spiritual beliefs. The body expresses what the soul impresses. Sacred dance is the people's way of impressing their spirits and bodies on the larger cosmos. To dance is not simply to express motor behavior but to inscribe or imprint on reality the presence of soul in the universe. Black sacred dance is a form of freedom, for it releases the body from the parameters of social and spiritual constraint. In other words—and this is particularly true for black

Americans living in closely knit quarters on plantations and in other forms of residential apartheid in America—the spirit of freedom had to be imitated and expressed through various means. Dance is not only an expression of black souls breaking free but a means of spiritually, relationally, and socially reconfiguring the externally imposed boundaries of oppression and restraints.

Put differently, to dance is to spiritually, culturally, and physically exceed the barriers and impediments of restraint socially imposed by a system of oppression, segregation, and domination. It is black souls and bodies transcending the walls of isolation and insulation created by oppression. Dancing is thus a sacred act of freedom urging black bodies and souls to extend beyond the predetermined perimeters and modalities of white cultural behavior and action. Dancing is, thus, not only emotional release, physical and psychological therapy, and cultural expression, it is also a movement of the body and souls into other realms of the cosmos, spheres not shaped or determined by human beings but by God.

As a form of spiritual and cosmic imprinting, it enables black people to connect with a higher spiritual reality. Dance is not a result of transformation but an act of spiritual transformation in worship. Dancing is a means of shaping the chaos of reality and putting the dancer in touch with the implements of personal transformation. The liturgies of black life are thus written through various forms of sacred black dance in worship and in the larger panoply of African American culture. Without politicizing all elements of black worship, I think it important to underscore the cultural and spiritual significance of black worship as a force for freedom and transformation. For too long the cultural and spiritual infrastructures of the black church have been negated as important elements of black freedom. It is precisely because the black church has developed a cultural and spiritual ethos where the freedom to interpret, express, and transform the black self in relation to divine reality has been so strong, that it has had such powerful influence on the African American paradigm of freedom.

For some, to affirm that shouting, praising, and dancing in black worship are not only expressions of human freedom seems misplaced. However, if we fathom how black spirituality has shaped black culture in the church, we can begin to appreciate how as forces for freedom they have influenced other areas of the African American experience. Suffice it, therefore, to say that dance, praising, or shouting are not simply personal emotional or cultural expressions. We must understand how the black church has created a context for the continual, pristine manifestation of black soul force as an element of religious belief and expression as well as an instrument of cultural and social transformation. That blacks have used the church to freely express the power of soul as a creative life force means it has had a major role in shaping black expectations, assumptions, attitudes, and behaviors about how culture and spirituality function as vital forces for human freedom.

Sacred dance has also had an important influence on how culture and spirituality could be used as stepping stones to freedom in American society. Freedom is not only experienced in the expression of dance itself but also in the expression of those modalities of belief and expression that are essential to free souls and spirits. Body and soul therefore coalesce into a liturgy and movement of sacred invocation, where those previously imposed social limitations and manacles are broken through dances of spiritual transcendence.

Singing and
Instrumental Music

Black worship is not only a celebration of life in the Spirit but also an affirmation of cultural and spiritual freedom. It is in the context of worship that ingredients, values, and forms of African American freedom are actualized and expressed. Singing and instrumental music are also important parts of the movement and celebration of freedom in black worship.

The black church has traditionally been the place where black musical creativity has been discovered, nurtured, and honed, where black people could freely experiment with more creative idioms and vehicles of musical expression. Much of current black music emerged from this ethos of creativity cultivated in the black church.

We stated earlier that jazz, spirituals, and gospel emerged from the black church under aegis of creative black spirituality. We might even venture to say that the blues, rhythm and blues, and some forms of rap emerged from the cultural repertoire of African American churches. The freedom to sing and create music reflecting the concerns, attitudes, culture, and reality of black life has been primarily nurtured in the African American church. No other institution has had the same influence on the formation and amalgamation of black culture and black spirituality. It is important to note that the black church was not only a creative oasis for new musical ideas but a catalyst for such creative expression by creating the context for black culture's full emergence and influence in the larger American arena. In other words, it was because black music and singing were shaped and honed under the influence of the black church that gave it both its unique style and legitimacy in the eyes of the larger culture and society.

Eileen Southern tells us that many of the musical gifts of black slaves were learned on their own and that slave festivals and celebrations were

places where those talents were showcased.[10] She further observes that
many of their musical abilities were retentions of Africa and that the development of various musical styles and expressions indelibly reflect
African influences. Accordingly, it was not until the black church con-
gealed as an institution with its own ritual dramas, practices, and traditions that it began to exert such strong impact on the musical ideas of
African Americans. The cultivation and nurturing of black soul force in
the black church is also significant. Whether it is the soul stirrings of
Aretha Franklin or the sheets of sound of John Coltrane, the black church
and black spirituality are pivotal influences in African American musical
styles and motifs.

We spoke earlier of improvisation and innovation as important elements of black culture manifested predominantly in black music. An
equally significant aspect is spontaneity, which is often found in black
worship services where an individual will break out into song on the glint
of the moment, leading the congregation in the service. Sometimes this
person is designated and sometimes not. At the entreaties and promptings of the Holy Spirit, music is soulfully shared in the experience of worship. The idea of cultural and spiritual freedom again emerges. Every
facet of worship is designed to exemplify or imitate the experience of letting the Spirit flow or being led by the Spirit in worship. This creative soul
force freedom is where believers come into intimate awareness of the
powers and workings of God, Christ, and the Holy Spirit. It is the power
of the soul to express and establish itself finally as a completely free entity.

In black worship one also finds other forms of instrumentation that express the freedom and power of the soul to discover, celebrate, and transform itself in worship. The use of organs, drums, guitars, saxophones, and
other instruments is not unusual in some black congregations. The point
is to celebrate God by whatever means available and to spiritually and
soulfully transport believers into different realms of reality. The capacity
to achieve such ends demonstrates the untrammeled spirit of a liberated
people. To move in the Spirit and be subsequently transported by it is an
attainment of remarkable value. The power to invoke the Spirit's presence
and to musically create idioms and media that reflect the creative motifs
of black culture and black spirituality is a salient aspect of African American freedom. Thus music can redress what politics cannot. The soul can
deeply express those dimensions of life and being that external social realities cannot.

In listening to black singers one invariably senses the essence of creative soul force. It may be found in the peculiar turnings or inflections of
a phrase or the way a song is sung. It may follow a predetermined script
but is largely ordered by the passions, feelings, and prompting of the

Spirit. Black singing has an unmistakable presence of soul passion, a feeling that stirs and moves the human spirit like no other singing. Evident then is a passion and freedom to interpret, express, translate, and transform the music according to the proclivities of the human spirit. This capacity to interpret, express, translate, and transform music in black worship is disclosed in every area of African American culture and life. The same freedom to determine and shape music according to the propensities of creative soul force is revealed in other aspects of black existence. What black people creatively do with music in worship and black culture, they also do in business, politics, education, athletics, science, and other realms of black existence. To embellish and punctuate reality with the presence of black soul force for sanity, dignity, and survival is an important element of black culture and spirituality and an essential construct in the African American paradigm of freedom.

Black worship, then, is the parental source of cultivating and flourishing such creative and free ideas. It is here that the creative use of culture and spirituality forge a common matrix of human freedom. If blacks can freely worship, improvise, innovate, and spontaneously create according to the promptings of the Spirit, they can also translate such freedom into other areas of their lives. The cultural and spiritual implements of black freedom are developed and honed in the black church and often experimentally presented in worship services. The foundation of African American freedom is thus located in the spiritual and cultural traditions of the black church and is evidenced in the way creative soul force is used as an instrument of spiritual and social transformation.

Identifying, expressing, nurturing, celebrating, empowering, and transforming creative soul force has been the central task of black spirituality and the black church. It is the single most important resource for African Americans in constructing and cultivating a unique paradigm of human freedom. Without creative soul force we would not have the black church, black culture, or those elements of black life and existence essential to sanity, dignity, and black survival in America.

Deliverance, Conversion, and Transportation

Whatever we say about various forms of black worship, a central assumption is not only spiritual and social transformation through creative soul force and the power of the Holy Spirit but *deliverance, conversion,* and *transportation.* Deliverance and conversion are elements of spiritual transformation. Believers will be delivered from the fowler's snare and empowered to live more productive and Spirit-filled lives. Conversion is a manifestation of transformation. All these experiences suggest a freedom of God to use black people according to the dictates and movement of God's Spirit.

Another salient feature of black worship to which we alluded earlier is the idea of black worshipers being transported into other spiritual realms. The freedom of God to move worshipers into spiritual and cosmic domains not privileged by their masters is also an important aspect of freedom in black worship. Being transported into other spheres of existence means that believers have a spiritual power to remove themselves from the confines of reality. While for some this may appear to be escape, for many it attests to the freedom of the soul to chart its own course and direction in conjunction with divine reality. Where black people have not been free to go socially and relationally, they have been free to go ethereally and spiritually. Again this is not an excuse but a basic fact of black existence. Worship is a time of letting go and finding other places to go in the movement and power of God's Spirit. This freedom to transport and be transported manifests a capacity that ultimately negates any human attempts to dominate, subjugate, and desecrate black life. "Swing low, sweet chariot, coming for to carry me home."

The focus here is on spiritual and even bodily movement away from the constraints and manacles of reality. The spirit is so attuned to incitement by the Holy Spirit that black believers regularly undergo out-of-body experiences where the spirit and soul of humanity vitally connects with God, resulting in conversion and deliverance! Thus it is not enough simply to move into other spiritual and cosmic realms of existence. One cannot return from such experiences the same person as one left. A basic presupposition is that conversion and deliverance are made possible by a genuine revelation of God and that the power of such an encounter transforms the consciousness and being of the believer into something new and vital. Thus deliverance is made possible by the revelation, and the revelation precedes spiritual transportation. Essential here is the radical participation of the human spirit in ways that create radical transformation of mind, body, and soul. Conversion, deliverance, and transportation are fundamental aspects of black worship and integral to ideas of human freedom in the African American experience.

Preaching, Teaching, and Reaching

Perhaps one of the most important rituals of African American worship is preaching, which has to do with teaching and reaching, and has always been the citadel of black freedom. Using imagination through the power of the Spirit to heal and transform black lives is a critical dimension of African American preaching traditions. Since the black preacher is both the embodiment and messenger of black freedom, black preaching is the means by which such freedom is interpreted, formulated, and espoused.

Preaching is the pinnacle of spiritual and cultural freedom in a predominantly oral culture, for words create their own litanies and liturgies of survival, dispense their own cures, and contain the power to radically transform black life. Perhaps no other idiom or medium has had more influence in shaping black consciousness, aspirations, and attainments than black preaching. How could black people hear without the black preacher?

Black preaching has been a dynamic cultural and spiritual force in the lives of African Americans. The power of the spoken word by the man or woman of God to the people of God is quite astounding. The message, praxis, and imperatives of freedom are often exemplified in black sermons. Such freedom is manifested not only in the content of the sermon but also in the way the sermon is constructed, interpreted, and delivered to black audiences. Whether it is the whoop or moan or simply flat-footed fiery elocution on the glories and powers of God, the black sermon is one of the most important elements of black spirituality and black culture.

Freedom is biblically based—for example, the exodus—and the broad expanse of hermeneutical freedom revealed in the imagination, construction, and verbalization of black sermonizing is equally important. That freedom is not only exemplified in the text, but the way that text is taken, interpreted, and explicated is equally significant.

Some black preaching has been criticized for taking hermeneutical license that is incongruous with the trajectories and assumptions of certain biblical texts. While some black sermonizing may lack of exegetical integrity, it usually remains true to the spiritual and existential experiences of black people. Henry Mitchell is helpful in citing the elements of a black hermeneutic that demonstrates the integrity of black preaching even if it does not always follow the hermeneutical norms of white culture.[10] The fact is black preaching has saved and transformed lives and is an important part of black worship, the black church, and black spirituality. Without it the black church and black people could not have come this far. Since the African American church is the center of freedom, and worship provides the context for the spiritual and cultural creation and expression of freedom, black preaching represents the apex of creative soul force in conjunction with the Holy Spirit, making it one of the most powerful idioms of freedom for black people in America. Black preaching heals, troubles, incites, calms, embraces, transforms, transports, translates, and ultimately helps black believers confront, surmount, and transcend the decimations and afflictions of their condition. It has always been a vital force for freedom in black life, for the black preacher was the only one who had the authority to interpret the black experience and disseminate black aspirations, spiritually, culturally, and socially.

The roles of the black preacher and the black sermon as messengers of freedom have not been historically confined to cultural and spiritual concerns. The harsh realities of black social and political existence and the necessities of external freedom have been the subjects of much black sermonizing. More than any other person in African American life, the preacher bridges the social and spiritual, the political and cultural realities into a framework for a viable theology. It is not sufficient simply to preach biblically on the sins of slavery and social degradation without addressing the sins of social ills and problems today. Preaching means teaching and reaching. It is not enough to allow black people to find, interpret, and express themselves in church culturally and spiritually through creative soul force, they must be encouraged to translate those concerns into viable programs for social and political freedom. The black preacher and black preaching have been instrumental in making this happen.

Black preaching then has healed lives, brought families together, comforted the afflicted and afflicted the comforted, been a catalyst for cultural, spiritual, and social freedom, and black institution-building, served as a force for the creative transformation of black communities, institutions, and the personal lives of African American people. No other medium has done more to help shape, interpret, and disseminate black claims and aspirations for black freedom than black preaching.

The Soul of Worship

The foregoing are the liturgical and sacred elements of African American freedom that have been developed and nurtured in the African American church and through various African American spiritual and cultural traditions. We have stated that creative soul force as the most important element in the African American paradigm of freedom is cultivated in the black church in relation to black spirituality and black belief. Such soul force has been the overriding source for black creativity and culture and is essential to black freedom.

The black church and black worship have thus provided the contexts and vehicles in which the ritual dramas of black freedom have been actualized and expressed. Prayer, shouting, healing, music, dancing, praising, delivering, and preaching have not only been historic expressions of spiritual and cultural freedom in black churches and worship but have equally been instruments of celebration, affirmation, translation, and transformation of the African American experience in totality. The cultural and spiritual basis of the African American paradigm of freedom that nurtures and cultivates creative soul force as an instrument of black expression and empowerment is fostered and honed in the African American church. Worship is the time and place where these values of culture, freedom, and spirituality are clarified and disseminated corporately.

Moreover, the significance and power of the black church and worship lie not only in providing an ethos in which black spiritual and cultural freedom can thrive but in helping black people translate those structures, modalities, assumptions, values, and beliefs of spirituality and culture into social and political freedom. Providing a foundation for translating and ritualizing these concerns into liturgies of survival and freedom is an equally important element of the black church, worship, and spirituality.

By providing an ethos in which the ritual dramas of black life can be corporately realized through these various idioms and expressions of black spiritual belief, the black church and worship create a context for ritualizing and sacralizing the ultimate concerns of black existence. Through praxis evolve regularity, routinization, uniformity, and custom, which establish and legitimate the various forms of spiritual expression. The black church and worship are places where those rituals are created, cultivated, and honed into sacred rites and ceremonies that confer value, power, and purpose on African American people.

Freedom is realized in the creative flourishing of black soul force as an implement of black culture and black spirituality; in the way black believers are encouraged to freely embody, express, and create spiritual praxis and belief in culture and worship; in the amalgamation, praxis, and translation of black spirituality and culture into social forms of freedom; and in the various ritual drama processes that value, legitimize, corroborate, and ultimately empower and transform the lives of African American people. To fathom freedom from an African American viewpoint, we must first comprehend how culture and spirituality blend into a unique matrix of creativity and power through creative soul force and how the black church and worship provide a context for the creative expression, interpretation, and dissemination of those ideas, values, behaviors, and beliefs that reinforce black freedom.

Because of spiritual and cultural freedom through soul force, African Americans have evaded all possibilities of complete social domination and subjugation by their masters. Black culture and black spirituality have served as strongholds of resistance to final and thorough annihilation by adversaries. The black church has been the place where black culture, black spirituality, and black soul force have happily merged into a creative force for spiritual, social, and cultural transformation in American society.

A central contention of this project is that because black people through creative soul have been free enough to pray, praise, shout, preach, create culture, and spirituality as viable instruments for the transformation of both personal reality and society, they have laid the foundation for social and political freedom. The great error has been using one measuring tape for freedom and uniformly applying it to all peoples at all stages of human history. The fact is there are different forms of freedom, all of which have variances and common elements.

Thus the African American paradigm of freedom uses black culture and black spirituality as creative forces for facing, maintaining, confronting, transcending, and transforming black reality and for this reason constitutes a unique model of freedom. It is the way the culture of oppressors has been used and wed with the various aspects of African culture, values, and spiritual beliefs that has created the unique aspects of the African American paradigm. Because the black church and worship have been instrumental in ritualizing a forum for the actualization of such freedom through the praxis of spirituality and culture, it has had consecrative and sacralizing value in the lives of African American people. Amid the forces of brutalization, devaluation, and dehumanization, black life has had a sacred purpose.

Seven

Soul Survivors

African American spirituality has empowered black Americans to be soul survivors amid the nefarious realities of racism, discrimination, and dehumanization. Contrary to conventional wisdom, African Americans have developed a unique model of human freedom. This paradigm is realized in the way African Americans have developed and practiced their spirituality as a foundation for creating and expressing culture and as a means for creating and transforming social reality. African American spirituality has created a context for the emergence of a culture of creativity engendered by creative and resistant soul force, which has enabled black Americans to interpret, confront, embrace, transcend, and ultimately transform the culture of the oppressors into a meaningful reality of soul survival.

The uniqueness of African American spirituality lies in how it has created an ethos that allows for the practice of human freedom through the varying expressions of soul force. Black spirituality has thus created a reality of vitality where the structures of consciousness and modalities of black behavior and belief have found creative and redemptive expression through the creation and development of African American culture. This capacity to create a soul force culture or black culture soul is the African American gift of freedom. While blacks have not been politically, socially, or economically free in American society, the practice of spirituality enabled them to develop various forms of internal, psychological, spiritual, and cultural freedom through the creation and expression of new ideas, through the intentional appropriation and synthesis of certain cultural elements of their oppressors with their African remnants, and through the capacity to name, interpret, embrace, and transcend the dominant cultural realities of their oppressors.

African American spirituality has thus allowed blacks to become soul survivors through the following:

- The creation of an ethos in which creativity and freedom of expression were allowed to flourish vis-à-vis social, political, and racial constraints, which made for a mind, spirit, and will that could embrace, reject, or transform social reality.

- The development of behavioral modalities and cognitive structures that encourage alternative expressions of thinking, seeing, and being in a racially oppressive society.
- The creation of a context of spiritual expression and vitality that allows for the creative use of culture as a means of expressing creative and resistant soul force and as a means for interpreting, confronting, embracing, and transcending current dominant realities.
- The creation of systems of healing, vitality, and meaning for personal and relational empowerment through the expression and use of a spirituality of culture and a culture of spirituality as a means of transforming the self and society.

African Americans have not been satisfied with simply creating spiritual and cultural models of freedom in lieu of political and social models. Because blacks were not free to live as their white counterparts—that is, socially, economically, and politically in American society—they had to create structures of consciousness and modalities of belief, behavior, and expression through culture and spirituality that allowed the soul and spirit to find freedom. In other words, African American spirituality allowed black Americans to create other models of spiritual and cultural freedom in a society when they were denied social and political freedom. Spiritual and cultural freedom of African Americans is the infrastructure and foundation to their struggle for social and political freedom in America. They found it insufficient, therefore, to create alternative models of cultural and spiritual freedom and simply be content. The task has been to translate the same creativity and modalities of alternative behavior and consciousness into the political and social realm in order to realize those external forms of freedom that have been largely denied.

African Americans have created a unique paradigm of freedom that allows for the creative expression of soul force both as a means of creating an alternative reality and culture as well as resisting those elements and remnants of the larger dominant culture that prevent African Americans from actualizing potential and realizing wholeness. Black spirituality has created the context for the development, emergence, expression, and preservation of soul force as a vital instrument for the development and transformation of African American life. This soul force is vital to personal, spiritual, and cultural freedom. Without it, black people could not have survived nor could they have created alternative models of being and consciousness that provide meaning, sanity, and well-being in a society determined to devalue and destroy them.

By permitting the expression and cultivation of creative and resistant soul force in African American churches, African American spirituality has created the ethos of mind that perpetually seeks alternative, ethereal forms of being and behavior that embrace and transcend, adopt and transform, accept and reject those forms of consciousness, behavior, and belief that reinforce the subjugation, devaluation, and ultimate annihilation of African American people.

Notes

Notes to the Introduction

1. This idea of the culture soul embraces the notion of spirituality as a creative force for culture.
2. Marimba Ani defines this as the vital force of a culture, set in motion by Asili. It is the thrust or energy source of a culture, that which gives it its emotional tone and motivates the collective behavior of its members. See *Yurubu* (Trenton, N.J.: African World Press, 1994), xxv.
3. "Strong Men," *The Collected Poems of Sterling Brown,* ed. Michael S. Harper (Chicago: Tri-Quarterly Books, 1989), 56.
4. From "Lift Every Voice and Sing," in *Songs of Zions,* ed. Edward B. Marks Music (Nashville: Abingdon Press, 1981).
5. Personal communication.

Notes to Chapter 1.
The Sources of African American Spirituality

1. This debate between Herskovits and Frazier set the stage for continuing polemics about this issue. The recent proliferation of black scholarship and the Afro-centrist movement has made the survival of Africanisms in the American experience axiomatic. For further information see E. Franklin Frazier, *The Negro Family in the United States* (Chicago: University of Chicago Press, 1966), 3–16; and Melville Herskovits, *Myth of the Negro Past* (Boston: Beacon Press, 1958), 1–19. See also, *Africanisms in American Culture,* ed. Joseph Holloway (Bloomington, Ind.: Indiana University Press, 1990).
2. See John Mbiti, *African Religions and Philosophies* (New York: Anchor Books, 1970), and *Introduction to African Religion* (Oxford: Heinemann International Books, 1975); E. Bolaji Idowu, *African Traditional Religion: A Definition* (Maryknoll, N.Y.: Orbis Books, 1975); Kwesi A. Dickson and Paul Ellingworth, eds., *Biblical Revelation and African Beliefs* (Maryknoll, N.Y.: Orbis Books, 1969).
3. See Albert Raboteau, *Slave Religion* (New York: Oxford University Press, 1980), 43–92. Raboteau distinguishes between various forms of African spiritual possession and the spiritual shouting traditions of African Americans. See Robert Hall, "African Religious Retentions in Florida," in *Africanisms in American Culture,* ed. Joseph Holloway (Bloomington, Ind.: Indiana University Press, 1991).

4. Hans Baer, *The Black Spiritual Movement: A Religious Response to Racism* (Knoxville: University of Tennessee Press, 1984).

5. Dona M. Richards, *Let the Circle Be Unbroken* (Trenton, N.J.: Red Sea Press, 1989), 5.

6. For further discussion see E. A. Wallis Budge, *From Fetishism to God in Ancient Egypt* (New York: Dover Publications, 1988), 144–76; *The Egyptian Book of the Dead* (New York: Bell Publishing, 1960), 74–107. See also Carlyle Fielding Stewart, III, "African Foundations of the Idea of the Holy," unpublished manuscript, 1993; James Bonwick, *Egyptian Belief and Modern Thought* (London: African Publication Society, 1983). Other scholars have entered the fray of this discussion, Yosef ben-Jochannan, Charles Copher, Cain Hope Felder, to name a few.

7. Anthony Browder, *Nile Valley Contributions to Civilization: Exploding the Myths* (Washington, D.C.: The Institute of Karmic Guidance, 1992), 86.

8. See Mechal Sobel, *The World They Made Together: Black and White Values in Eighteenth-Century Consciousness* (Princeton, N.J.: Princeton University Press, 1989).

9. W. E. B. Du Bois, *The Souls of Black Folk* (Greenwich, Conn.: Fawcett Books, 1961), 16–17.

10. Marimba Ani, *Yurugu* (Trenton, N.J.: African World Press, 1994), 279–80.

11. Robert Bellah, *The Broken Covenant* (New York: Seabury Press, 1975).

12. *Selected Poems of Langston Hughes* (New York: Random House, 1987), 275.

Notes to Chapter 2.
The Spiritual Dynamics of African American Freedom

1. Invariably all discussions regarding black freedom in America focus on emancipation from external political and social power structures. Seldom does analysis underscore models of internal spiritual and mental freedom that prevented complete enslavement and domestication of black people by whites. It is precisely this emphasis on the internal spiritual aspects of liberation through the practice of spirituality and the creation of black culture that makes the African American paradigm of freedom unique.

2. Howard Thurman, *Jesus and the Disinherited* (Richmond, Ind.: Friends United Press, 1969), 56.

3. Ibid., 51.

4. Ibid., 81.

5. Robert McAfee Brown, *Religion and Violence* (Philadelphia: Westminster Press, 1973), 34–38.

6. Ibid., 28.

Notes to Chapter 3.
Living Freely and Spiritually

1. Dona Marimba Richards, "The implications of African American Spirituality," in Molefi Asante and Kariamu Asante, eds., *African Culture: The Rhythms of Unity* (Trenton, N.J.: African World Press, 1990), 216.

2. Ibid.

3. Geneva Smitherman, *Talkin' and Testifyin': The Language of Black America* (Detroit: Wayne State University, 1977), 77.

4. Lerone Bennett, *The Challenge of Blackness* (Chicago: Johnson Publishing Company, 1992).

5. James Baldwin, *The Fire Next Time* (New York: Reed, 1962).

6. James Baldwin, *Nobody Knows My Name* (New York: Dell Publishing, 1961), 70.

7. Creigs Beverly, "Spirituality: Oft the Missing Link in African-American Mental Health" (paper presented at Wayne State University in Detroit, Michigan in 1994).

8. Thomas Kochman, *Black and White Styles in Conflict* (Chicago: University of Chicago Press, 1981), 29–30.

9. Richards, "Implications of African American Spirituality," 208–9.

Notes to Chapter 4.
Spirituality and Freeing Relationships

1. Okechukwu Ogbonnaya, "Person as Community: An African Understanding of the Person as Intrapsychic Community," *Journal of Black Psychology* (February 1994): 79.

2. Ibid., 78.

3. Evan M. Zeusse, "Perseverance and Transmutation in Traditional Religion," in *African Religions in Contemporary Society,* ed. Jacob K. Olupona (New York: Paragon House, 1991), 173.

4. Geneva Smitherman, *Talkin' and Testifyin': The Language of Black America* (Detroit: Wayne State University, 1977), 82–83.

5. Henry Louis Gates, Jr., *The Signifying Monkey* (New York: Oxford University Press, 1988), 74.

6. Smitherman, *Talkin' and Testifyin',* 58.

7. Conversation with an elderly female parishioner at Hope United Methodist Church, Southfield, Michigan.

8. Joseph L. White, *The Pscyhology of Blacks: An Afro-American Perspective* (Englewood Cliffs, N.J.: Prentice-Hall, 1984), 3–4.

Notes to Chapter 5.
Spirituality and Cultural Freedom

1. James Haskins and Hugh F. Butts, *The Psychology of Black Language* (New York: Hippocrene Books, 1973), 39.

2. Howard Paige, *Aspects of African American Cookery* (Southfield, Mich.: Aspects Publishing, 1987).

3. John Miller Chernof, *African Rhythm and Sensibility* (Chicago: University of Chicago Press, 1979), 169.

4. J. H. Kwabena Nketia, *The Music of Africa* (New York: W. W. Norton, 1974), 27, 29.

5. Leroi Jones, *Black Music* (New York: Quill, 1967), 11–14.

6. Francis Bebey, *African Music: A People's Art* (New York: Lawrence Hill Books, 1975), 3.

7. See Howard Thurman, *Deep River and the Negro Spiritual Speaks of Life and Death* (Richmond, Ind.: Friends United Press, 1975); James Cone, *The Spiritual and the Blues* (New York: Seabury Press, 1972).

8. Eileen Southern, *The Music of Black Americans: A History* (New York: W. W. Norton, 1971).

9. Jon Michael Spencer, *Protest and Praise: Sacred Music of Black Religion* (Minneapolis: Fortress Press, 1990).

10. Cone, *The Spiritual and the Blues*; Henry Mitchell, *Black Belief* (New York: Harper & Row, 1975); Gayraud Wilmore, *Black Religion and Black Radicalism* (Maryknoll, N.Y.: Orbis, 1989); Theo Witvliet, *The Way of the Black Messiah* (Oak Park, Ill.: Meyer Stone Books, 1987).

11. Joseph R. Washington, Jr., *Black Religion* (Boston: Beacon Press, 1964), 206–7.

12. Thurman, *Deep River*, 83.

13. Cone, *The Spiritual and the Blues*, 108–9.

14. Leroi Jones, *Blues People* (New York: Quill, 1963), 50–59.

15. Samuel Charters, *The Roots of the Blues: An African Search* (New York: Perigee, 1981).

16. Cone, *The Spiritual and the Blues*, 109.

17. Jon Michael Spencer, ed., "The Theology of American Popular Music. A Special Issue of Black Sacred Music," *Journal of Theomusicology* (Fall 1989): 23.

18. Ibid., 26–29.

19. Ibid., 22.

20. Margaret Just Butcher, *The Negro in American Culture* (New York: New American Library, 1956), 40.

21. John Reilly, ed., *Twentieth-Century Interpretations of* Invisible Man (Englewood Cliffs, N.J.: Prentice-Hall, 1970); Jones, *Black Music*, 17–49.

22. Kathy J. Ogren, *The Jazz Revolution* (Oxford: Oxford University Press, 1989), 13.

23. Ibid., 11–12.

24. Ibid., 111.

25. Ibid., 12–13.

26. Ibid., 13.

27. Marshall Stearns, *The Story of Jazz* (New York: Oxford University Press, 1958), 3–15.

28. See Sule Greg Wilson, *The Drummers Path* (Rochester, Vt.: Destiny Books, 1992); Ashenafi Kebede, *The Roots of Black Music* (Tallahassee, Fla.: An Ethius Book, 1989).

29. Ogren, *The Jazz Revolution*, 12.

30. Carlyle Fielding Stewart, III, *Street Corner Theology* (Nashville: John Winston Publishers, 1996), 60.

31. We cannot overestimate the reality of improvisation in African American life. It has been a central unifying and creative force in African American spirituality and culture. Improvisation symbolizes creativity, the power of individuals

to transcend the limitations imposed upon them by the larger culture. It is the power to create and exist under conditions of nominal subsistence.

32. Wyatt T Walker, *Somebody's Calling My Name: Black Sacred Music and Social Change* (Valley Forge, Pa.: Judson Press, 1992), 15–26.

33. Edward Jones, *The Black Diaspora: Colonization of Colored People* (Seattle: Edward L. Jones and Associates, 1989), 129–41.

34. Carlyle Fielding Stewart, III, *African American Church Growth: Twelve Principles for Prophetic Ministry* (Nashville: Abingdon Press, 1994), foreword by Charles G. Adams.

35. See E. Franklin Frazier, *Black Bourgeoisie* (New York: Free Press, 1957), and Nathan Hare, *The Black Anglo Saxons* (Chicago: Third World Press, 1991).

36. Mason Brewer, *American Negro Folklore* (New York: New York Times Quadrangle Books, 1968); Langston Hughes, Arna Bontemps, eds., *Books of Negro Folklore* (New York: Dodd, Mead, & Co., 1958).

37. Bernard Bell, *The Afro-American Novel and Its Tradition* (Amherst, Mass.: University of Massachusetts Press, 1987); Gayl Jones, *Liberating Voices: Oral Tradition in African American Literature* (New York: Penguin Books, 1991); Addison Gayle, Jr., *The Way of the New World: The Black Novel in America* (New York: Anchor Press, 1976); Larry Neal, *Visions of a Liberated Future* (New York: Thunder Mouths Press, 1989); Henry Louis Gates, Jr., *Figures in Black: Words, Signs, and the "Racial" Self* (New York: Oxford University Press, 1987).

38. Richard Wright, *Native Son* (New York: Harper & Row, 1940); James Baldwin, *Go Tell It on the Mountain* (New York: Dell, 1953); Ralph Ellison, *Invisible Man* (New York: Vintage Books, 1947); Langston Hughes, *The Best of Simple* (New York: Hill & Wang, 1961); Toni Morrison, *Song of Solomon* (New York: New American Library, 1977).

39. Creigs Beverly, "Spirituality," 3.

40. See James Cone, *God of the Oppressed* (New York: Seabury Press, 1975) and Howard Thurman, *Jesus and the Disinherited* (Richmond, Ind.: Friends United Press, 1969).

41. Franky Kofsky, *Black Nationalism and the Revolution in Music* (New York: Pathfinder Press, 1970), 9.

42. Ibid., 65–66.

Notes to Chapter 6.
Spirituality and Freedom in Worship

1. Melva Wilson Costen, *African American Christian Worship* (Nashville: Abingdon Press, 1993), 49.

2. Henry Mitchell and Nicholas Cooper Lewter, *Soul Theology* (San Francisco: Harper & Row, 1986).

3. Costen, *African American Christian Worship*, 19–20.

4. Ibid., 18–19.

5. John S. Mbiti, *The Prayers of African Religion* (Maryknoll, N.Y.: Orbis, 1975), 14–15.

6. Aylward Shorter, *Prayer in the Religious Traditions of Africa* (New York: Oxford University Press, 1975), 1.

7. Ralph Wiley, *Why Black People Tend to Shout* (New York: Carol Publishing, 1991), 1–2.

8. Albert Camus, *The Myth of Sisyphus* (New York: Random House, 1955), 21.

9. Herbert Marcuse, *One Dimensional Man* (Boston: Beacon Press, 1964).

10. Eileen Southern, *The Music of Black Americans* (New York: W. W. Norton, 1971), 3–59.

11. Henry Mitchell, *Black Preaching* (Nashville: Abingdon Press, 1990).

Bibliography

Abraham, W. E. *The Mind of Africa.* Chicago: University of Chicago Press, 1962.

Ani, Marimba. *Yurugu.* Trenton, N.J.: African World Press, 1994.

Aptheker, Herbert. *American Negro Slave Revolts.* New York: International Publishers, 1968.

Asante, Molefi. *Malcolm X as a Cultural Hero and Other Afro-Centric Essays.* Trenton, N.J.: African World Press, 1993.

———, and Kariamu Asante. *African Culture: The Rhythms of Unity.* Trenton, N.J.: African World Press, 1990.

Baer, Hans. *The Black Spiritual Movement: A Religious Response to Racism.* Knoxville: University of Tennessee Press, 1984.

Baldwin, James. *Go Tell It on the Mountain.* New York: Dell Publishing Co., 1953.

Baldwin, Lewis. *There Is a Balm in Gilead.* Minneapolis: Fortress Press, 1991.

———. *To Make the Wounded Whole.* Minneapolis: Fortress Press, 1992.

Barndt, Joseph. *Dismantling Racism.* Minneapolis: Augsburg Press, 1991.

Bebey, Francis. *African Music: A People's Art.* New York: Lawrence Hill Books, 1975.

Bell, Barnard, *The Afro-American Novel and Its Tradition.* Amherst, Mass.: University of Massachusetts Press, 1987.

Beverly, Creigs. "Spirituality: Oft the Missing Link in African-American Mental Health." Wayne State University School of Social Work, 1995.

Billingsley, Andrew. *Black Families in White America,* Englewood Cliffs, N.J.: Prentice-Hall, 1968.

———. *Climbing Jacob's Ladder.* New York: Simon & Schuster, 1992.

Blackwell, James E. *The Black Community: Diversity and Unity.* New York: Harper-Collins, 1991.

Blassingame, John. *The Slave Community.* Oxford: Oxford University Press, 1970.

Bonwick, James. *Egyptian Belief and Modern Thought.* London: African Publication Society, 1983.

Brewer, J. Mason. *American Negro Folklore.* New York: New York Times Quaddrangle Books, 1968.

Brown, Sterling. *The Collected Poems.* Edited by Michael S. Harper. Chicago: Tri-Quarterly Books, 1980.

Budge, E. A. Wallis. *The Egyptian Book of the Dead.* New York: Bell Publishing, 1960.

———. *From Fetishism to God in Ancient Egypt.* New York: Denver Books, 1988.

Butcher, Margaret Just. *The Negro in American Culture.* New York: New American Library, 1956.

Camus, Albert. *The Myth of Sisyphus.* New York: Random House, 1955.

Charters, Samuel. *The Roots of the Blues.* New York: Perigee, 1981.

Chernof, John Miller. *African Rhythm and Sensibility.* Chicago: University of Chicago Press, 1979.

Cone, James. *God of the Oppressed.* New York: Seabury Press, 1975.

———. *The Spiritual and the Blues.* New York: Seabury Press, 1972.

Costen, Melva Wilson. *African American Christian Worship.* Nashville: Abingdon, 1993.

Dickson, Kwesi, and Paul Ellingsworth, eds. *Biblical Revelation and African Beliefs.* Maryknoll, N.Y.: Orbis Books, 1969.

Dixon, Christa K. *Negro Spirituals from Bible to Folk-Song.* Philadelphia: Fortress Press, 1976.

Driver, Tom. *The Magic of Ritual.* San Francisco: HarperCollins, 1991.

Ellison, Ralph. *Invisible Man.* New York: Vintage Books, 1947.

Evans, Anthony. *Are Blacks Spiritually Inferior to Whites?* Wenonah, N.J.: Renaissance Publications, 1992.

Felder, Cain Hope. *Troubling Biblical Waters.* Maryknoll, N.Y.: Orbis Books, 1989.

———, ed. *Stony the Road We Trod.* Minneapolis: Fortress Press, 1991.

Foucault, Michael. *Power/Knowledge: Selected Interviews and Other Writings 1972–1977.* New York: Pantheon Books, 1980.

Franklin, V. P. *Black Self-Determination.* New York: Lawrence Hill Books, 1992.

Frazier, E. Franklin. *Black Bourgeoisie.* New York: The Free Press, 1957.

———. *The Negro Family in the United States.* Chicago: University of Chicago Press, 1995.

Freire, Paulo. *The Politics of Education.* Granby, Mass.: Bergin & Garvey Publishers, 1985.

Gates, Henry Louis, Jr., *Figures in Black: Words, Signs, and the "Racial" Self.* New York: Oxford University Press, 1987.

———. *The Signifying Monkey.* New York: Oxford University Press, 1988.

Gayle, Addison, Jr. *The Way of the New World: The Black Novel in America.* New York: Anchor Press, 1976.

Harding, Vincent. *There Is a River: The Black Struggle for Freedom in America.* New York: Random House, 1983.

Hare, Nathan. *The Black Anglo Saxons.* Chicago: Third World Press, 1991.

Haskins, James, and Hugh F. Butts. *Psychology of Black Language.* New York: Hippocrene Books, 1973.

Hitchens, Melvin. *The Black Family in Marriage: A Black Man's Perspective.* New York: Welstar, 1993.

Hughes, Langston. *The Best of Simple.* New York: Hill & Wang, 1961.

Hughes, Langston, and Arna Bontemps, eds. *Book of Negro Folklore.* New York: Dodd, Mead & Co., 1958.

Hutchinson, Earl Ofari. *The Assassination of the Black Male.* Los Angeles: Middle Passage Press, 1994.

Idowu, Bolaji E. *African Traditional Religion.* Maryknoll, NY: Orbis Books, 1975.

Jones, Edward. *The Black Diaspora.* Seattle, Wash.: Edward Jones Associates, 1989.

Jones, Gayl. *Liberating Voices: Oral Tradition in African American Literature.* New York: Penguin Books, 1991.

Jones, Leroi. *Black Music.* New York: Quill, 1967.

———. *Blues People.* New York: Quill, 1963.

June, Lee N. *The Black Family: Past, Present, and Future.* Grand Rapids: Zondervan Publishing Company, 1991.

Kardiner, Abram, and Lionel Ovesey. *The Mark of Oppression.* New York: World Publishing Company, 1969.

Kebede, Ashenafi. *The Roots of Black Music.* Tallahassee, Fla.: An Ethius Book, 1981.

Kochman, Thomas. *Black and White Styles in Conflict.* Chicago: University of Chicago Press, 1981.

Kofsky, Frank. *Black Nationalism and the Revolution in Music.* New York: Pathfinder Press, 1970.

Kovel, Joel. *White Racism: A Pyschohistory.* New York: Columbia University Press, 1984.

Levine, Lawrence. *Black Culture and Black Consciousness.* Oxford: Oxford University Press, 1977.

Long, Charles. *Significations, Signs, Symbols, and Images in the Interpretation of Religion.* Philadelphia: Fortress Press, 1986.

Mbiti, John. *African Religion and Philosophies.* New York: Anchor Books, 1970.

———. *Introduction to African Religion.* Oxford: Heinemann International Press, 1975.

Mellon, James, ed., *Bullwhip Days.* New York: Avon Books, 1988.

Mitchell, Henry. *Black Relief.* New York: Harper & Row, 1975.

Mitchell, Henry and Nicholas Cooper Lewter, *Soul Theology.* San Francisco: Harper & Row, 1986.

Morrison, Toni. *Song of Solomon.* New York: New American Library, 1977.

Myrdal, Gunnar. *The Challenge of World Poverty.* New York: Vintage Books, 1970.

Neal, Larry. *Visions of a Liberated Future.* New York: Thunder Mouths Press, 1989.

Nkeita, J. H. Kwabena. *The Music of Africa.* New York: W. W. Norton, 1974.

Nobles, Wade. *African Psychology.* Oakland, Calif.: Black Family Institute, 1986.

Ogbonnaya, A. Okechukwu. *On Communication Divinity: An African American Interpretation of the Trinity.* New York: Paragon House, 1994.

———. "Person as Community: An African Understanding of the Person as an Intrapsychic Community." *Journal of Black Psychology* 20 (February, 1994): 75–87.

Ogren, J. Kathy. *The Jazz Revolution.* New York: Oxford University Press, 1989.

Olupona, Jacob K. *African Traditional Religions in Contemporary Society.* New York: Paragon House, 1991.

Paige, Howard. *Aspects of African American Cookery* (Southfield, Mich.: Aspects Publishing, 1987).

Park, Robert. *Race and Culture.* New York: The Free Press, 1950.

Patterson, Orlando. *Freedom in the Making of Western Culture.* New York: Harper-Collins, 1991.

———. *Slavery and Social Death.* Cambridge, Mass.: Harvard University Press, 1982.

Raboteau, Albert J. *Slave Religion.* Oxford: Oxford University Press, 1978.

Richards, Dona Marimba. *Let the Circle Be Unbroken.* Trenton, N.J.: Red Sea Press, 1989.

———. "The Implications of African American Spirituality." In *African Culture,* ed. Molefi Asante and Kariamu Asante. Trenton, N.J.: Africa World Press, 1990.

Rosseau, Jean-Jacques. *The Social Contract and Discourse on the Origin of Inequality.* New York: Washington Square Books, 1967.

Rutstein, Nathan. *Healing Racism.* Springfield, Mass.: Whitcomb Publishing, 1993.

Smitherman, Geneva. *Talkin' and Testifyin': The Language of Black America.* Detroit: Wayne State University Press, 1977.

Smith, Wallace Charles. *The Church in the Life of the Black Family.* Valley Forge, Pa.: Judson Press, 1988.

Sobel, Mechal. *The World They Made Together: Black and White Values in Eighteenth-Century Consciousness.* Princeton, N.J.: Princeton University Press, 1989.

Somé, Malcolm Patrice. *Ritual Power: Healing and Community.* Portland, Ore.: Swan/Raven Company, 1993.

Southern, Eileen. *The Music of Black Americans.* 2d ed. New York: W. W. Norton, 1971.

Spencer, John Michael. *Protest and Praise: Sacred Music of Black Religion.* Minneapolis: Fortress Press, 1990.

Staples, Robert. *The Black Family.* Belmont, Calif.: Wadsworth, 1986.

Stearns, Marshall. *The Story of Jazz.* New York: Oxford University Press, 1958.

Stewart, Carlyle Fielding, III. *African American Church Growth.* Nashville: Abingdon Press, 1994.

———. "The Black Church: Paragon of Strength for African-American Families." Paper presented at Spaulding Institute in Detroit, Michigan, February 23, 1993.

———. *God, Being and Liberation: A Comparative Analysis of the Theologies of James Cone and Howard Thurman.* Lanham, Md.: University Press, 1989.

———. *Street Corner Theology.* Nashville: John Winston, 1996.

Stuckey, Sterling. *Slave Culture.* New York: Oxford University Press, 1987.

Swan, L. Alex. *Survival and Progress: The African-American Experience.* Westport, Conn.: Greenwood Press, 1981.

Thurman, Howard. "America in Search of a Soul." Paper presented on January 20, 1976.

———. *Deep River and the Negro Spiritual Speaks of Life and Death.* Richmond, Ind.: Friends United Press, 1975.

———. *Jesus and the Disinherited.* Richmond, Ind.: Friends United Press, 1949.

———. *With Head and Heart.* New York: Harcourt, Brace, Jovanovich, 1979.

Turner, Victor. *The Ritual Process.* New York: Cornell Paperbacks, 1969.

Walker, Wyatt T. *Somebody's Calling My Name: Black Sacred Music and Social Change.* Valley Forge, Pa.: Judson Press, 1992.

———. *The Soul of Black Worship.* New York: Martin Luther King's Fellow Press, 1984.

Washington, Joseph R., Jr. *Black Religion.* Boston: Beacon Press, 1964.

Watts, Alan. *The Wisdom of Insecurity.* New York: Vintage-Pantheon Books, 1951.

West, Cornell. *Prophesy Deliverance.* Philadelphia: Westminster Press, 1982.

White, Joseph. *The Psychology of Blacks*. Englewood Cliffs, N.J.: Prentice-Hall, 1984.

Whitehead, Alfred North. *Adventures of Ideas*. New York: The Free Press, Macmillian Company, 1961.

Wilmore, Gayraud. *Black Religion and Black Radicalism*. Maryknoll, N.Y.: Orbis Books, 1989.

Wilson, Sule Greg. *The Drummer's Path*. Rochester, Vt.: Destiny Books, 1992.

Witvliet, Theo. *The Way of the Black Messiah*. Oak Park, Ill.: Meyer Stone Books, 1987.

Wood, Forrest. *The Arrogance of Faith*. New York: Alfred A. Knopf, 1990.

Wright, Richard. *Native Son*. New York: Harper & Row, 1940.